The First Information Is Almost Always Wrong

150 *THINGS TO KNOW ABOUT*
Workplace Investigations

BY MERIC CRAIG BLOCH, ESQ., CCEP, PCI, CFE

Printed in the United States of America.
18 17 16 15 14 13 12   1 2 3 4 5 6 7

ISBN: 978-0-9792210-6-4

The views expressed in this book are those of the author. They do not necessarily
represent the views of his employer or any third party.

This publication is designed to provide accurate and authoritative information
in regard to the subject matter covered. It is sold with the understanding that
neither the authors nor the publisher are engaged in rendering legal, accounting, or other professional service. If legal advice or other expert assistance is
required, the services of a competent professional person should be sought (from
a Declaration of Principles jointly adopted by a Committee of the American Bar
Association and a Committee of Publishers).

To order copies of this publication, please contact:

Society of Corporate Compliance & Ethics
6500 Barrie Road, Suite 250, Minneapolis, MN 55435
PHONE *+1 952 933 4977* | FAX *+1 952 988 0146*
www.coporatecompliance.org
service@corporatecompliance.org

To my Mother
The person who taught me the things I needed to know

CONTENTS

PART II—Protect Your Company: How to Integrate Your Investigations into Your Company's Operations

PART IIII—Protect Your Case: How to Conduct an Effective Workplace Investigation

Introduction

"This is the business we've chosen."

In *The Godfather 2*, Hyman Roth, an aging Jewish gangster patterned after the famous Meyer Lansky, makes the statement quoted above to Michael Corleone, head of the now-powerful Corleone organized-crime family. The two had been discussing the murder of a rival gangster, and Roth understood that the killing was necessary despite his personal affection for the victim. Roth's point was that their occupation imposed on them certain realities and limitations. Death was an occupational hazard. Killing was part of their business operations.

Well, workplace investigations are the business I have chosen. Perhaps you've chosen it too. But it seems that workplace investigations are done often, but not well. Opportunities to make a significant contribution are routinely missed. There are just too many mediocre investigators—like re-purposed human resources managers and all-too-confident lawyers who believe that workplace investigations are so straightforward and simple that their past professional experience instantly prepares them to investigate misconduct. If you want to be one of these people, stop reading now.

People have described me both as an institutional heretic and profession-ally sarcastic. It wasn't always this way. When I was hired as a compliance officer and started conducting investigations full time, I naturally thought I would be welcomed into the corporate family and given a seat at the man-agement table. It was not my first job, however, so I expected to encounter the inevitable turf battles and ego-driven manager struggles. But I figured that managers would support me because they needed the information I could develop to enable them to deal with the employee-specific and operational problems investigations usually identify.

Wrong. I quickly learned that "I'm from Compliance, and I am here to help" doesn't exactly persuade colleagues to support you. In hindsight, I shouldn't have been surprised. The head of Human Resources thought I was taking a bite out of her empire and was convinced misconduct investigations should remain within her group. The lawyers were welcoming—I guess I still knew the secret handshake from my earlier years as an in-house attor-ney—but they could not imagine a need for my investigation skills because of their own well-considered talents. Other departments were more or less accommodating, but these people considered me fairly irrelevant to their job duties. In short, despite my good efforts and even better intentions, I was not welcomed with open arms.

After having been fired from my last job as part of a corporate house-cleaning following the replacement of that company's general counsel, I was determined not to place my professional future in the hands of my colleagues. So while I developed my investigative skills as the volume of my investigations grew, I polished my skills as a corporate ambassador, salesman and publicist. I saw each investigation as an opportunity to showcase to the business people the value of a thorough inquiry. I used the investigation as an opportunity to develop allies and advocates among the business executives. But, deep down inside, I was doing everything I could to justify my continued employment. I would not rely on others to uncover my value.

Friedrich Nietzsche wrote "That which does not kill us makes us stronger." Well, my secret motivation and marketing efforts made me stronger. After hundreds of investigations and even more sales-pitches, I have learned a lot. From interviewing techniques to dealing with hostile executives, from defending against allegations made against me—there's no defense for an implicated employee like a good offense—I endured hundreds of teachable moments. So I thought it was time to assemble these thoughts and pass along some of the most important ones.

The compliance industry is relatively new, but it is still mature enough for us to demonstrate our value. Using the investigation process to showcase the value of the compliance program depends completely on our ability to conduct a meaningful, business-oriented investigation. But where can you turn for help? There seem to be few books out there giving practical guidance to people who conduct workplace investigations. The available materials seem to focus either on traditional human-resources investigations—I call them the "I hate my boss" cases—or are written by lawyers for other lawyers who handle bet-the-farm investigations over allegations that risk destroying their corporate clients. I hope that this book will help fill the knowledge gap for the remaining 80 percent of the cases we handle.

This book reflects some of what I learned through conducting hundreds of workplace investigations, ranging from traditional personnel matters to multimillion-dollar fraud investigations. This book gives you practical guidance from someone who, to paraphrase, attended the investigative school of "hard knocks." This book is about the gritty part of the compliance business. This book is not about philosophy, ethics or feel-good messages like "tone from the top." I will leave those areas to others. Someday, perhaps, I will be able to contemplate those topics in depth and find ways to solicit nodding heads of approval from other compliance professionals.

For now, I remain in the rough-and-tumble of corporate life, trying to do an important job as best I can—probably like you—while trying simultaneously to remind everyone that my continued employment is in our collective interest. If you are in the same position, please keep reading. Although it is good to learn from your mistakes, it's better—not to say smarter—to learn from someone else's. I hope you will read this book carefully and learn from what I have done both right and wrong. This information is not about high moral principles. It is presented as professional and personal advice from one investigator to another.

This book is organized in three parts. The first, and most important part, discusses your professional survival. The second part discusses how to integrate successfully your investigative efforts into your company's operations. The third part discusses how to conduct an effective workplace investigation that adds maximum value to your company.

For convenience, this book uses the masculine form for pronouns although, of course, women are equally capable investigators (and implicated people of investigation). Similarly, references to a "company" or a corporate setting can be equally applied to any organization.

Meric Craig Bloch
Livingston, New Jersey

PART ONE

Protect Your Career:
How To Think Like a Workplace Investigator

For all the value and insights an investigation may contribute to a company, much depends on the skills and efforts of the investigator assigned to that case. An investigator, however, cannot contribute much—for this case and future ones—if he becomes collateral damage to the investigation.

There is no sure-fire way for an investigator to protect against accusations of improper investigative conduct. Considering the nature of the matters investigated and the consequences for employees committing misconduct, an investigator always risks accusations of misconduct. An investigator should do everything reasonably possible to reduce this risk. Fortunately, there are a number of protective steps an investigator can take.

1) Never say always. Never say never.
Everyone's job inevitably falls into patterns—or ruts: the doctor who sees patients all day during flu season with the same symptoms; the plumber who unclogs sinks every day; the accountant completing zillions of similar returns during tax season. Investigators are no different, but we need to resist taking a cookie-cutter approach to our work.

It may be your umpteenth my-boss-hates-me investigation, but there will always be some detail to make this case different from the others. The variables are always there to make the investigation unique.

Don't make assumptions about how the investigation will ultimately affect the people involved because, despite what might have happened in the past, you cannot be certain until all the facts are in. Making assumptions poses two risks to both you and the investigation. First, it closes off your mind to other possibilities and explanations. For example, if you assume that one of the implicated colleagues did nothing wrong, then you might miss the information that implicates him. The assumption becomes like putting on blinders. You'll ignore the information that does not fit within your intellectual template.

The second risk is that you might assure an upcoming witness that he's done nothing wrong, only to have him implicate himself later in his interview. What are you going to do then, especially if the witness then says your earlier statements tricked him into saying something incriminating? There is nothing wrong with telling someone that, at that point in time and subject to additional information that could show something different, it does not appear that he's done anything wrong. But always give yourself wiggle room, and say "It doesn't appear" rather than "I don't believe." The proof counts here, not what you think may have happened.

An investigation frequently ends in a different place than where you thought it would when your efforts began. Sympathetic witnesses turn out later to be arrogant tyrants to co-workers, and vice versa. People who initially appeared innocent of any wrongdoing are later found at the center of the misconduct. What seemed like a discrete act of misconduct turns out to be a pattern of problems in that department. Theories and colleagues implicated (or vindicated) may change.

So don't lock yourself, either internally with your thinking or externally with others, into early conclusions. Don't pre-judge the outcome of an investigation before all the witnesses have been interviewed and all the relevant documents have been reviewed. Use the issues and your working hypothesis as general boundaries that can be crossed as the information you develop warrants.

Keep an open mind to other possible explanations or scenarios. Go where the facts take you. You will be frequently surprised where they eventually lead. A genuine inquiry requires asking lots of questions and observing. Making assumptions too early will also make you look either like a know-it-all or patronizing.

You weren't there, so you can never be entirely sure what happened. Keep all your investigation options open. Never say never, and never say always.

$2)$ You aren't collecting for the Red Cross and this isn't an audit. But you aren't the Prince of Darkness either.

You can regularly describe yourself as a business advisor helping to identify unacceptable business risks. And this does play well when advocating the investigation process internally. But when you are assigned a case, how will you position yourself to the people affected by the allegation? What are you going to say in order to set the stage for effective fact-finding?

You have a bit of a dilemma. Do you, figuratively speaking, kick in the door and announce that you are conducting a misconduct investigation? Or do you use the subtle "I'm just trying to understand the facts" approach?

Different cases require different approaches. It will be up to you to choose the right one. Whatever you choose, have no illusions.

Investigations disrupt workplaces. A misconduct allegation arises, and the next thing people see is an investigator snooping around the department asking lots of questions. No matter how professional and objective you try to be, you will still get dogged by the stereotypes and preconceived notions about investigators. Everyone thinks that, behind your statements of "I am just a company employee too," lurks a second-guessing finger pointer searching for some reason to blame people.

At times, you will get frustrated. Your frustration, coupled with your desire to have productive fact-finding, may give you the urge to mask your true role as a company investigator. Perhaps such a suggestion will come from the business executives who want to minimize the disruption of your presence. You might think it's an easier way to accomplish your goals. But whatever the source of the idea, resist the temptation.

Credibility is essential to an investigator. You'll never be able to tell everyone exactly what they want to hear—for example, that you're sure nothing will happen to them for "borrowing" from the petty cash fund—but you do control whether people believe what you tell them is accurate and truthful. When you mislead people, for even what seemed like a reason that helps the company, you are effectively telling everyone that they should not rely on your statements or intentions. Before you even ask your first interview question, you've already told them not to trust you.

So when these business-disruption and similar process concerns arise, tackle them directly. Investigations are a normal part of any company's internal operations. Investigations are one of the ways the company polices itself. There is no need to describe your presence as serving some other purpose, like quality control or an audit. There is no need to portray your role as anything other than protecting your company by investigating a report of actual or suspected misconduct.

This approach makes the most sense if you encounter resistance from the implicated person. Most initial reports—and the allegations that spring from them—are not fabricated. The facts described likely occurred in one form or another and your job is usually to determine whether those facts are actually misconduct. (For example, an investigation into whether an off-color joke was discriminatory usually proves easily that the joke was told, regardless of its consequences for the joke teller.) So if one of the actors in the underlying facts tries to resist cooperating, he must be gently reminded both that the investigation is a regular business function as well as the logical consequence of his actions.

Just as you shouldn't mislead people as to your role, remember that you aren't the Prince of Darkness either. There are a number of unflattering stereotypes for investigations, all of which may undermine your credibility and effectiveness. The ability to strike fear in your colleagues will not yield useful information. Instead, it leads witnesses to lie, evade and generally recollect nothing. Once again, you are just doing an important job for your company by finding the true facts of what happened.

You aren't their friend, but you're not their enemy either. Don't let people label you. Don't label yourself either.

3) Be infamous. Investigations can be a dirty business.

Just as you shouldn't mislead others as to your true purpose, don't fool yourself either about the nature of workplace investigations. You should market your function internally as simply another part of the company's risk-management operation. You can emphasize how detailed inquiries actually protect the company by identifying areas of unacceptable business risk. You can bring value to the company by conducting investigations both offensively (to determine where problems occurred and how) and defensively (to identify facts which help minimize your company's liability). You can do everything you can think of to showcase your business value.

But when all is said and done, accept the reality that people frequently get fired once the investigation is done. Business people generally get blamed for allowing a subordinate to commit misconduct, even though that manager didn't even know it was occurring. The police sometimes get called and, from time to time, former employees go to jail. These are not the regular outcomes of most other business functions.

Your must also acknowledge that the best thing that can happen to a colleague who assists you in an investigation is nothing. The witness or implicated person isn't getting a bonus, promotion or likely even a "thank you" for cooperating. Investigations can be a dirty business—few internal business processes cause grown men to cry during regular business meetings—and we need to accept this reality as professionals.

So accept that people may be intimidated and scared. And if not of you personally, then they will be scared of what you do. Don't think that, as time goes on and you complete more investigations, people will become less scared because you have become a more-defined quantity in your company. The opposite may be more likely. People will learn that you are sufficiently skilled to get to the bottom of things and find out what truly happened. It will become more unlikely that—to the discomfort of some—you would just throw up your hands in frustration, walk away from the matter, and conclude that the true facts could not be determined.

So be infamous if you must. Anyone would prefer to be loved and admired by his colleagues. But it isn't likely to happen to investigators. Switch professional disciplines if you crave the cheers and accolades of your leaders and co-workers. You're not likely to be chosen as the "Employee of the Month" when an important milestone for your career will be the first time your workplace investigation leads to the criminal indictment of a now-former employee.

4) All the ideals you believe in are true, even if they aren't always evident.

I'll leave it to others to decide whether an investigator is better off being idealistic or cynical about human nature. My guess is that perhaps somewhere in the middle is best.

Workplace investigations focus on what goes wrong in your company and not what goes right. You'll rarely investigate the high-fliers who are taking your company to new levels of business success. You will become more acquainted with the people at the other end of the talent and job-performance spectrum. The issues you confront often offend your own sensibilities. It may be hard at times to imagine someone in your company being so daring, amoral or indifferent. Over time, you may develop a thick skin either to shield your own values or to abandon them professionally.

Don't lose your ethical bearings or your sense of right and wrong. Most employee decisions you investigate are made, quite frankly, by foolish or incompetent people and not evil ones. Their decisions are usually motivated either by short-term goals or short-term thinking. And even these people usually just made a succession of what-was-I-thinking errors that were compounded by later attempts to conceal earlier decisions.

You probably do work for a good company with good people. For the most part, the reasons you joined these people are still there. Unfortunately, the nature of your job won't let you see too much of that. Try to keep your perspective. It stinks, but your job does not allow you the luxury of idealism.

5) Forget being invited to Christmas parties.

Corporate cultures generally encourage the integration of all the company's employees, regardless of department, into one big family. You always see company newsletters showing a picture of the CEO chatting with the mail-room guys at the holiday party.

Conducting workplace investigations seems different from other company functions because it is different. We look into employee and process failures. We identify where things went wrong. It's probably a nice environment in which to make a living, but we don't operate in the part of the company studded with corporate slogans and the latest business fads. We can't solicit smiles and high-fives by cajoling colleagues with magnets, key chains and stress balls. When was the last time there was a "Company Investigations Day" in your cafeteria with free cake for everyone?

We routinely handle highly confidential, serious subjects. Although we collaborate with colleagues in other departments, the implications—stereotypical and realistic—of our work cannot be ignored. People frequently get fired. The police may be called. Lawsuits may start, and customer relationships may end.

With all of this going for us, it's no surprise that people try to keep us at arms' length. It is also a professional fact of life that investigators cannot necessarily be on the same team as everyone else in the company (or others may not perceive them to be). Our effectiveness and independence depends on keeping some detachment from our co-workers. Expect this to extend beyond the boundaries of a particular investigation.

So don't pretend your job choice doesn't have consequences. This should make you realistic, not cynical, about the line of work you've chosen. Just don't expect to be invited to many Christmas parties (unless your bosses want you to keep an eye on people there).

6) Do the right thing, even if it is not convenient.

Investigators face their own ethical issues. Our work generally gives us flexibility, autonomy, self-direction, discretion, and minimal oversight. This gives us the latitude to do our jobs well, but it also creates an opportunity for trouble.

You are responsible for protecting your own ethical health. No investigation is worth risking your integrity and future effectiveness—not to mention your continuing employment—for the sake of determining what exactly happened in a particular case. When you get frustrated, feel unappreciated or misunderstood, or are laboring under a heavy workload, it can be tempting to cut corners and rush to judgment to close the investigation. This temptation rarely comes from poor professional values. The temptation might come from a confidence in "rough justice" so that the implicated person gets what he so richly deserve. Whatever your motivation, resist it. There is almost always a proper way to achieve the same objective. (And if there isn't a proper way, you can't do it.) Ethical lapses among investigators result more from laziness, frustration and a lack of imagination than from the lack of a more-ethical alternative.

The most common ethical lapses for investigators include:
- Violating the privacy of the people involved.
- Disclosing confidential information when it was not essential to do so.
- Using deception as an investigative technique, such as lying or playing with someone's emotions.
- Coercing people to "roll over" on their colleagues.
- Promising something in exchange for a witness's cooperation.

These things have no place in a professional workplace investigation. These examples are helpful because they show how mundane the lapses can be. (You don't see extortion, slander, or false imprisonment among the lapses listed.) The point is that it is the little things that will take you beyond ethical boundaries. It also underscores why your professional standards must be kept high. You can avoid problems like the appearance of impropriety by remaining self-aware of your actions and statements. It takes a little more effort to stay on the straight and narrow, but it is worth it in the long run.

As the old saying goes, a clear conscience makes the softest pillow. So when your findings lead to someone's dismissal, you'll know that the person received a fundamentally fair investigation.

7) It's business, so don't take things personally.

Investigations frequently lead to employee discipline, termination or pros-ecution. Expect emotions to run high. Witnesses cry during interviews. Others enter damage-control mode, either denying everything or over-whelming you with trivial nonsense. Even innocent people will panic if they fear a witch-hunt. In return, people might accuse you of trying to ruin their jobs so you can collect another employee scalp for your wall. Each of these emotions will be directed at you.

Don't take outbursts personally. It is not about you. You represent the power of the company. You embody those possible negative consequences. So you are the one on whom the fears are projected.

Stay detached and focused on your job. Be self-aware of your statements and actions. Keep alert to the perceptions you create. You might not be able to change their feelings, but don't enable them either.

8) You are not the morality police.

Workplace investigators often earn their stereotypes. We do not strive to conduct effective and business-oriented processes. We often take the path of least-resistance—let's show Bob stole the money, close the case, and let the bosses fire him—rather than critically examine the perfect storm of factors involved. Some investigators enjoy acting like morally superior avenging angels. Their investigations second-guess the actions of those who are actually trying to make money for our companies. These investigators fail to manage perceptions and cultivate management allies.

Don't make your professional life more difficult than it has to be. You are part of the company's risk-management apparatus, not an avenging angel. Position yourself as a business advisor and promote that message instead. Make your findings business-related intelligence rather than something like a police report. When you change how you portray your role, and you help your colleagues improve the business by identifying and solving problems, they will change their perceptions too.

You control how others perceive you and your function. Control the perceptions well.

9) You're damn right I did.

Despite best practices and a focus on improved techniques, workplace investigations are an inexact science. For example, it is considered a best practice for companies to establish investigative protocols, but even on the best days these can be little more than a set of default standards. Each investigation is a unique mix of allegations, contributing factors and personalities. And within personalities come individual agendas and psychology.

Over time, each investigator develops a standard approach to doing things. The approach usually grows from experience and reflects what has worked over time. A good investigator defends his investigation technique by developing a preventive armor. This armor can be summed up as "you're damn right I did." When conducting an investigation, interviewing people, and discussing matters with management, keep a sixth sense about what you are saying, what you are doing, and the likely impressions you are leaving. It is almost as if you were observing your own conduct. Don't say or do anything that you are not prepared to explain—to a witness, your boss, the CEO, or an outside company lawyer—the details that show how it was in the best interests of both the company and your investigation goals. Remain prepared to explain and professionally justify whatever you did or didn't do.

So, some time in the future, when your boss turns to you and asks: did you really ask that witness if she and her boss were romantically involved, you can reply "you're damn right I did," and then explain why. The bottom line for personal accountability in the investigation process is that if you can't take ownership like that for something you want to say or do, then you shouldn't say it or do it.

10) Be objective.

You are a professional. Never collect evidence to suit a preconceived notion of guilt or some other desired outcome. First, this will blind you to other possible explanations of the conduct you are investigating. Second, if the allegation can be substantiated, the proof you develop will show that without the need for you to boost it with your assumptions.

Investigators are fact-finders. You don't get paid extra for the number of scalps on the wall. Find the facts, and you will find the truth. Where there is blame to be assigned, the truth can do it sufficiently well without your assistance.

11) You have to be "pro-investigation."

As an investigator, you are neither neutral nor an ombudsman. You are a management representative. But although you are a management representative, you are not pro-management. If the relevant managers seek a certain result, but the facts you develop do not justify it, they must be denied the result they seek.

You may not be pro-management, but you are not pro-cop either. You seek to determine what happened so your organization can operate better and management changes, if needed, can be made. You are not a police officer, and the arrest of an implicated employee rarely helps the bottom-line of a company.

You are also not pro-colleague. The person you investigate may be despised by their department colleagues, and the investigation may give them a feeling that karma will finally deliver to this person what he so richly deserves. But if the facts do not justify it, they must too be denied.

But you are pro-investigation. You are part of the company's risk-management system. You seek to protect the interests of the company and the rights of those colleagues involved in your view. The only way you do this is through a professional effort, based on experience, training and an ethical approach to your fact-finding.

12) The only good faith you can bet on is yours.

After enough investigations, you start getting a bit jaded. You feel that you only encounter what goes wrong in your company. You never seem to be on the side of the company that gets awards, high-fives and invitations to those all-expenses-paid trips to the Bahamas. Instead, people get fired, someone always winds up in tears during their interview, and no one benefits from working with you on an investigation.

You try to keep the human touch, so reporters are often the first people in an investigation to gain your sympathy. They tell you compelling stories about someone else's outrageous behavior or unfairness. The problems they describe created a toxic atmosphere in the office. The pattern continues with other colleagues. By the time you are finished interviewing the witnesses, you are perplexed how such an awful co-worker (or boss) has avoided his comeuppance until now.

A sense of humanity is crucial for any investigator. Not only do you need a human touch when dealing with others—a key to soliciting valuable information—you need to see the humanity in them. But be careful that your capacity for humanity doesn't mean you reflexively accept their characterizations or their impressions of the potential misconduct. Doing that would effectively mortgage the credibility of your investigation to the veracity of your reporter and witnesses. Balance the need for skepticism with appropriate sensitivity.

So keep your humanity and accept theirs. Gather the information you get from them, but don't assume anyone's good faith. Judge everyone's credibility, and remember that even bad-faith reporters can be telling the truth. Only the facts you develop in the investigation will prove whether the reporter is truly aggrieved and a good corporate citizen, or a vindictive character assassin looking for your help to settle some past score. Don't get sidetracked because someone tugged at your sympathies or your sense of fair play.

13) Keep control of the investigation from the beginning to the end.

When a serious allegation of misconduct arises, the business people involved simultaneously react to a number of concerns. There is the implicated employee who was previously in a position of trust. There may be an unhappy customer that now has a "crisis of confidence" in your company's ability to perform. There may be executives who the business people fear will blame them for allowing the problem to occur. The implicated employee may be a sales superstar who the department managers fear losing to the competition. These factors usually lead to business people trying to steer the investigation towards their particular goals and away from their professional fears.

Ownership of an investigation comes from the pride that is taken in conducting the most complete and objective review as professionally possible. Ownership comes from adhering to a set of guidelines and principles, rather than politics and situations. The ultimate objective of an investigation is a full inquiry that is not motivated by politics, personality or expediency.

These principles can be tested when the urgencies of a critical situation arise. But adhering to them at such times becomes more important than ever. Establish your role at the outset as the "quarterback" of the investigation. Leave no doubt with your colleagues that the company places the investigative responsibility with you. Whatever their motives are for wanting to take such an active role, it is you, not they, who remain accountable to the company for a successful, professional and proficient investigation. Investigation-by-committee simply does not work.

When people seem to be interfering with your investigation, ask yourself why these people seek such an active role. You'll quickly find that their motives are understandable and usually practical. They are likely motivated by a fear of what the investigation will show, and how they may be blamed by their superiors. If this happens, don't get into a wrestling match with them about the investigation. Instead, explore why they feel they need such an assertive role—instead of just being the customer of your efforts. You may find you can accommodate their needs fairly easily, and they will step aside and let you do your job.

There is room in the investigative process for others to participate—indeed, this is the best way to keep it business-focused—but it is you, not they, who have the training and responsibility for completing the investigation. Solicit their needs and concerns, and then do your best to respond to their priorities. Help where you can. Make sure you understand their post-investigation needs. But you must personally set the strategy and decide what has to be done to complete the investigation. You own the process and its outcome.

14) You are responsible for a good investigation, no matter who helps you.

Sometimes, you conduct all parts of the investigation yourself. In other cases, certain tasks, like interviewing minor witnesses, are delegated to colleagues in other departments. Everyone enjoys having help to make their job easier, but it can be a mixed blessing. Regardless of how many people are involved in your investigation, you still own all of it. You are ultimately accountable, from everyone from the reporter to the Board of Directors for the successful outcome of the investigation and every task you delegate. It will never be sufficient to blame a poor effort by someone else as simply your error in trusting them to be competent.

Read and review every investigation memo, every piece of evidence and each document. Make sure you know what has happened and remains to be done. Understand a colleague's interview goals before the interview happens. If something does not seem kosher, fix it immediately. Stay on top of things. Never put yourself in a position where you mortgage the quality and integrity of your investigation—and possibly your reputation—on the diligence, understanding and skill of someone else.

15) Perceptions can be reality.

The credibility of an investigation is tied to yours. If your efforts are not obviously professional and objective, any investigation result will be tainted. This is true even if something merely appears to be wrong, even though the true facts are otherwise.

Just as the investigation can become tainted, so can the investigator. For example, be alert to any actual or perceived conflicts of interest. Avoid even the appearance of bias or partiality to a particular person or result. If you believe that an actual or perceived conflict exists—such as if you know the people involved in some way—that might compromise your objectivity or you have some interest in the matter being investigated, stop and inform your supervisor immediately. The integrity of the process requires that someone else conduct the investigation. You control the perceptions, so manage them well.

Perceptions quickly become reality. Stay sensitive to how things look.

16) Everyone second-guesses themselves. You will too.

Workplace investigations are not template company processes. Each one is somehow unique, so there will always be investigative options you didn't consider. Or options that, with the benefit of hindsight, would have yielded a better result had you taken them. Frequently, you'll realize either that you should have asked one more question that would have been the clincher to get that confession, or you'll regret the question you shouldn't have asked which then caused the implicated person to clam up because he realized he had already told you too much.

Learn from both your successes and mistakes. Treat your workplace investigations as a continuous learning process. Second-guessing is healthy (as long as you don't project your doubts to others). Introspection reflects both your desire to improve your professional competence and your appreciation of the practical impact of your findings. Just don't let critiques preempt you from being bold when you need to be. Self-analysis will progressively lead you to be a better investigator.

17) Don't look for a bad guy. You probably won't find him. If he is there, he will find you.

Misconduct occurs more often because of the failures of human nature rather than the failures of business processes. Misconduct results from ignorance, negligence, poor training, inadequate supervision or a failure to consider the consequences of some step taken. And when you look closely, you'll see that the mistakes are rarely stupid ones. Mistakes are usually made by business managers based on the perception of their immediate environment and the decisions they made. The crisis then comes as a result of the decision's unintended consequences. Actions taken even for good reasons might have collateral results that were neither intended nor foreseen.

Don't unintentionally hamstring your investigation by searching only for evildoers. Despite the excitement of an investigation to smite evil from your company and an understandable desire to act on the side of the angels, most workplace investigations are less glamorous. Even when misconduct is substantiated, the misconduct may be unintentional.

Looking only for the "bad guy" among your implicated employees may be a fool's errand. That person is going to be the exception among your investigated colleagues. So unless you are sure it's something worse, assume it was not intentional misconduct like fraud and theft. If the motives turn out to be more sinister than you expected, the investigation will bear that out.

The "bad guys" do exist in your company. But when faced with a choice between incompetence and intentional misconduct, bet incompetence every time.

18) You can't be a genius in every investigation. Try anyway.

Take your job seriously. Cultivate a passion for investigating. Get specialized training to increase your effectiveness. Don't become complacent in your work. Each investigation has some aspect that makes it unique, and there is always the chance for a teachable moment if you look closely. Find that moment and use it to improve your craft. You, the company, and your co-workers will be better off for it.

Get proper training. Never rely on accumulated past habits or professional conceit—"I'm a lawyer so of course I can handle an investigation"—as the basis of your claimed competence. You'd never want your doctor to treat you as a learning experience, and your colleagues—especially those with their jobs at risk—don't want you to do it either.

Most investigators are generalists, and the breadth of their experience tends to reflect the fact that most cases involve human-resources issues. What are you going to do when an investigation is needed in a more-specialized area like workplace fraud?

Increase your utility and expand your investigation competence. Buy a book or take a course. Grab a webinar off the Internet. Don't just wade into the new area unprepared. While it is true that you cannot be a genius in every investigation, give yourself as much knowledge as possible. The good news is that most investigations, regardless of the context, follow the same basic steps. In time, you might become a genius in that area, too. It's often the little details that distinguish one type of investigation from another.

It can be tough to work and learn at the same time. But all you can do is your best, with the time and resources you can fairly devote to your investigation. Strive to be a genius—remember to better yourself—but accept that you cannot be a genius in every investigation. But be aware that the time you encounter something particularly challenging in an investigation may be when you realize you should have acquired that knowledge earlier.

19) Don't tell anyone about past investigations.

If you work for a large company, it is unlikely that you will encounter the same people—witnesses or implicated employees—in later investigations. You will mostly see new faces with each case. However, it is possible that an implicated person in an earlier investigation will pop up in a later case.

It would be one thing if the earlier investigation substantiated the allegation against the employee (and assuming he was disciplined without being fired). Then the finding could be discussed among a key group of people because maybe the new allegation shows a pattern of conduct about which the company should be concerned. It might now also justify the implicated person's termination. (Of course, the prior investigation does not free you from meeting your burden of proof in the current one.) But what do you do if the earlier investigation cleared the implicated person? Should you mention it?

Consider a practical example. Assume you are investigating a company executive. A few years earlier, the two of you had a "professional interaction" when you had to investigate an anonymous report against him that he was flirting with his female subordinates and pursuing an office romance. Although office gossip had it that the executive regularly flirted with women in the office, you could not substantiate the allegation.

In the second investigation, assume a similar allegation was made. The executive was now working in a different company division but his reputation—now more urban legend than reality—travelled with him. Assume the executive's boss, new to the company but having been there long enough to hear stories, is trying to gauge the potential damage and asks you if any allegations like the current one had been made in the past. What should you do?

This creates a dilemma. The existence of a past allegation is a matter of fact, regardless of whether it was ultimately substantiated. If you mentioned the investigation, you wouldn't be saying anything that wasn't true. And shouldn't the boss know that the executive got jammed up before? After all, you could also explain how the executive was cleared of the allegation, and wouldn't that actually help the executive in the eyes of his boss?

It may be best to express no comment about an earlier investigation when the implicated person had been cleared. What are important are the current allegation and its possible impact on the business. Even if you explained the earlier investigation with all the right words and disclaimers, you cannot prevent the boss from presuming guilt and concluding that your finding in the last investigation had more to do with your investigation skills than the implicated employee's innocence.

So what do you do in the second investigation? Say nothing to the boss other than that, as a matter of professional practice, you do not comment one way or the other about past investigations. The first allegation is immaterial. That investigation is closed, and guilt in the second investigation cannot be presumed simply because a similar (although unsubstantiated) allegation arose earlier. Stay focused on the current allegation and its possible impact. Keep the boss focused there, too.

20) Turn misconduct into knowledge.

What happens in your company when someone reports an incident of actual or potential employee misconduct? Does your company respond to the report to investigate the situation, remedy it or learn from it? Or does your company treat the report as little more than a disposal problem that arises from time to time only to delegate the report *ad hoc* to a human resources manager or in-house attorney to handle (in addition to their regular duties)? Does the outcome, even assuming the investigation gets completed, even matter to them? How serious is the company about learning what may have happened?

If you work for a successful company, there is no doubt that it assesses risks all the time. Checks are run on new customers to determine if they are credit-worthy. Aging reports are prepared for accounts receivable to determine if the risk of non-payment has reached unacceptable levels. Before a new branch office is opened, decisions will be made whether the risk that it will be unprofitable is less than the possibility of financial success.

But what about the business risk from employee misconduct? What about the vulnerabilities of company systems—not to process inefficiencies or mediocre operations—but rather to fraud and abuse? Is anyone looking into those areas of risk besides you? These risks affect shareholder value, too. If protecting the investments of your owners is a primary duty of each company employee, identifying and addressing those risks with a thorough investigation places our function squarely within the business's fundamental purpose.

All of this reasoning sounds fairly straightforward, so why doesn't every company's management adopt such an enlightened approach to using investigations? It may be that management believes the company does not have the time, personnel or resources to conduct investigations efficiently. Executive management may think that the value of a workplace investigation is intended only to substantiate the misconduct of a single employee, and that the business leaders are already certain of his guilt. It may also be that management's approach is to "let sleeping dogs lie," and ignore problems that are known to exist but seem too disruptive and costly to fix. It may be they have a lack of imagination to see the business value of a thorough inquiry. It may be that your managers are too confident in their own high-minded ethics message to consider that a robust investigation might be a way to confirm that the message is as effective as they hoped it would be.

Whatever got your managers to this point is irrelevant. What matters is that both your effectiveness and professional success depends on you broadening their perspectives. And it's not like they haven't been conducting investigations until now. Even before Compliance Departments existed, companies have assigned corporate-security departments or human resources people or retained lawyers to look into allegations of wrongdoing. But the goals there are not the examination of business processes and corporate counseling. (Their purposes are, respectfully, threats to company assets, personnel management, evaluation and advocacy of applicable legal interests.) There is a world of difference when you use the investigation process as a way to improve business processes and as a risk-management tool, rather than when you use it only as a way to prove that a discrete act of misconduct occurred.

Let's be even more practical. Substantiating employee misconduct is comparatively easy. With at-will employees, little is needed to justify their termination. This sets the bar fairly low for investigation quality. Consequently, almost anyone can conduct an investigation. As a professional investigator, you should push the bar higher. You can do that by using the allegation as an opportunity also to identify process and management failures, and other areas of unacceptable business risk.

Think big and share your thoughts. Don't be complacent and accept your company's—probable default—position on limited inquiries. Act like the corporate fiduciary you are, and squeeze more value from your work. Help your company turn misconduct into knowledge.

So help your company by helping yourself. It's a win-win situation.

21) Be a reality therapist and an organizational pathologist.

Investigators are often criticized for not helping a company's profit-making goals. The criticism is frequently deserved. We ask lots of questions in order to explain whether the misconduct actually occurred. If we develop enough facts, the implicated person is disciplined or terminated. If we don't, then the investigation is closed, and life goes on. Too often, we stop there.

An investigator is an organizational pathologist. When you conduct a business-focused investigation, you will do more than assemble the gathered facts into a coherent narrative. Because misconduct always has a personal dimension, you'll explain it. For example, you won't just report that expense-reimbursement requests were processed without the requisite manager approvals, in violation of your company's financial controls. You'll also explain the rationale that allowed the misconduct to happen: that the department manager considered sales the most important part of his job because his bonus depended on it. Consequently, the manager never even reviewed expense reports before signing them because he considered them an unnecessary distraction from what he believed were the company's higher priorities.

In other words, don't limit the investigation to just answering the question. Try to understand the problem fully. Use your professional imagination. Consider the company's bigger needs. Help explain the dysfunctional department and its interpersonal dynamics. Illustrate the personal motives and goals at work. Show how a business process spelled out on paper either does not achieve its desired goal or is ignored altogether. Explain the reality of the situation you investigate and the perfect storm of factors that created it. Dissect the troubled situation and make some sense out of it.

22) There will always be blood on the floor. Don't be squeamish, but don't enjoy it either.

Few factual allegations are unsubstantiated. The initial report shows there is usually some problem, even if its contours aren't clear. A fabricated allegation is rare, so the investigation often turns on proving the implications of certain employees' conduct rather than the existence of it. Even if the original allegation cannot be substantiated, most investigations nevertheless uncover some wrongdoing (it might have been the same misconduct only characterized inaccurately), and this usually leads to someone getting fired. Face it: your efforts facilitated someone's termination. If you work to empower business managers to exercise their authority fully, some of that authority will be used to fire people.

It would be easy to paint a nasty look on your face and pretend that the implicated people are just getting what was coming to them. After all, no one held a gun to their heads and made them sexually harass their assistants. And all you did was identify the facts that were already out there, right?

In corporate life, heads usually roll when something goes wrong. (As companies disingenuously say, implicated people leave "to explore other options outside the company.") This outcome can happen even to the people your investigation connected tangentially to the problem.

You'll encounter more people who made bad choices than those who are evil. You should take professional satisfaction in successfully explaining what happened and proving misconduct actually occurred, but that satisfaction should never extend to enjoying that someone lost his job or got severely disciplined. After all, that poor schnook might have deserved to get canned, but he probably has a wife and kids. Chances are they are already suffering for his bad decisions.

When you lose your humanity, ask your boss for a transfer to another department. You'll never be as effective in your current position as you once might have been.

23) Your company has a legal obligation, but you have a moral obligation to the employee.

There are two grades in investigations: A and F. "Good enough" is rarely the standard for true professionals, even when work burdens must to be prioritized among limited time and resources.

Investigations require you to be as precise as possible. An investigation may preserve a colleague's reputation or destroy it. Managers rely on your fact-finding to make decisions about personnel, internal processes and management accountability. But the legal obligation is satisfied if the company conducts even some minimal inquiry. But that minimum threshold should be irrelevant to you. Do you really want someone's job affected by your desire to get the case wrapped up as quickly as possible? Do you want to live with the fact that you could be wrong? Take the time and do it right.

Try your best to get admissions of fault from the implicated person in your investigation. Admissions make some of the best proof you can gather. Even the employee who admits taking the money without permission but always intended to pay it back when his financial situation improved is still telling you he stole it. (The only difference is the characterization, and he doesn't get to decide which characterization is right.) Then whatever happens, you only identified and documented his wrongdoing; you didn't need to presume it from circumstantial proof.

When all you have is a circumstantial case—the employee denies any wrongdoing, but the developed facts certainly support it—then do your best to assemble as complete a case as you can. Process fairness requires you to identify any conflicting or mitigating information. You want the clearest possible picture of what happened.

Whether it is a reflection of your professionalism or your desire to avoid a guilty conscience for reaching the wrong conclusion by cutting corners, take the time to do it right. If you are going to fulfill this role in your company, you have a moral obligation to everyone involved to do your best possible work.

24) Beware the iceberg.

The initial discovery of misconduct is sometimes just a symptom of a much larger problem in the affected department. Keep alert to the possibility that what looks initially like a report of discrete misconduct may actually be a sign of a bigger, more troubling problem. (This also gives you an opportunity to expand your investigation and contribute some real value.)

Investigators also seem to be the last one to learn of seemingly ubiquitous facts in a company department, so you may be the last to know about some endemic problem in your company. Be prepared to expand your investigation questions accordingly. Remember the tip of the iceberg.

25) When interviewing, remember that no case is more important than your personal and professional safety.

Investigations are provocative things. Consider your personal and professional safety when a location is chosen. Witnesses can be unpredictable, especially when, during the fact-finding stage, you don't know much about them or what they may have done. Similarly, they don't know you and how your efforts may affect them.

Desperate people do and say desperate things, including when their careers may be on the line. So never take an interview in a place, such as a hotel room or car, where you might be accused of doing or saying the wrong thing to a witness. Have witnesses drive their own cars to interview locations, or take a taxi together. It takes little for a witness to try to undermine the investigation by accusing you of improper behavior (and he may not have a lot to lose at that point). And then it will fall to you to prove what you DIDN'T do. (The witness might also make a later claim to play the "litigation lottery" against your company.)

Much of this risk can be avoided if you use common-sense precautions. Ask a trusted colleague to monitor the interview to corroborate, if necessary, that your conduct was proper. If the implicated person is likely to be terminated based on your investigation as soon as the interview is complete, perhaps it might be best to be on your way to the airport before the person gets told he's being fired. Similarly, never give out any personal information, especially information about your home address. Remember that you are the tip of the spear in the disciplinary process. Managers will routinely explain to the employee that your investigation is what requires his termination. This makes you the bad guy and the source of the implicated person's pending misfortune.

An ounce of prevention here can prevent problems later on.

PART II

Protect Your Company: How To Integrate Your Investigations Into Your Company's Operations

Investigators don't work in a vacuum. Ours is just one of multiple staff functions in the company. This means that workplace investigations, besides the goals of any specific investigation, must improve company operations and protect shareholder value. How you accomplish these objectives and showcase your contributions may determine your success.

26) The bosses drive the bus.

The economics of capitalism and private enterprise favor risk taking. Identifying those risks places a goal of the investigations process squarely within the business's fundamental purpose. This presents us with an opportunity. But there is a boundary each investigator must respect.

You will usually be the one with superior knowledge of the facts. But insight is not the same as authority. You cannot substitute your judgment for those who run the company. You can explain facts. You can identify the risks. You can answer questions as they arise. But once you've done your job, the decision, along with accountability for its consequences, rests with the bosses. We are only advisors. Once the facts are sufficiently delivered, our work is essentially done.

From time to time, the bosses will disregard your information in favor of an approach you didn't advocate. (For example, they may want to compensate a customer fully in a loss for which your investigation determined the customer was at least partially at fault. Or a decision will be made to retain a misbehaving sales executive although your findings clearly justified his immediate firing.) Accept also that you may not always be able to influence executive decision-making as much as you'd like. You are a business advisor, not a decision-maker. Leave decisions to the people who are both empowered to make them and are held accountable for their consequences.

27) The quality of your compliance program is decided internally, not externally.

Investigators and their compliance colleagues frequently judge the quality of their efforts with comparisons to what other investigators and compliance people do in their own companies. We think that if we implement a similar hotline, if posters are also in every lunchroom, if we "borrow" a cool slogan from another company, if we hand out wallet cards with information, or if we have quarterly compliance-council meetings, then our company has a top-notch program because all the bases seem covered. But this is the wrong, if understandable, approach. Your company leadership decides whether you are valuable, not the other attendees at a compliance industry conference.

Your value depends on the substance you contribute, not the processes you implement. When you help management with their problems, and they know it, then they will support you. The opportunity is there for you if you are willing to go look for it. There is no doubt that this approach is a harder effort than just mimicking others' approaches. But an honest assessment is worth it. Have the courage to face the judgments and value calculations offered by the people who pay your salary. Don't settle for abstract considerations that may work for other companies, yet don't consider your true worth to your company.

28) Don't be just another layer of bureaucracy.

You may think you contribute something meaningful to the company's bottom line, but do you really? And if you are confident that you do, do others see that value?

Investigations are the place where "the rubber meets the road" in the compliance process. The other compliance steps are proactive and abstract rather than operating within a factual context of actual employee misbehavior. The goal of these steps is to channel and foster future employee behavior and not focus on already-occurring conduct.

Good investigators favor substance over process. When reporting on investigation details and findings, senior compliance people get to describe their company's compliance function in glowing terms, when all they may have done is repackage and recycle an investigator's efforts and push the results upward. Even if the investigation were done well, these people don't necessarily add value to it.

Bottom line: Contribute your own substance, whatever your role in the compliance function. Your company already has enough process.

29) Know how typical managers truly think.

Business leaders generally don't see the benefits of investigations as part of the process of running a business and reducing unacceptable risk. This is unfortunate, and we are partially responsible for this perception. Often an investigation's scope and findings are not made relevant to the world in which business people operate. One way to achieve relevance is to understand how business people think so you can tailor your efforts accordingly. So let's consider some of the realities of the business world:

First reality: Business people are hired—and fired—depending on their ability to generate revenue for the company. Compliance programs are not profit centers of a business, so the mere existence of a Compliance Department doesn't help them too much. Unless you have something to say that has a bottom-line significance, many business people probably won't care too much about what you do. Your function then is not perceived as essential to their business success, and they'll focus resources on the functions that do.

Second reality: The lack of involvement of most business managers in structuring Compliance Departments leads to confusion about the proper role of ethics in business (beyond just slogans and unquestioning certainty about an important but abstract role). Compliance isn't intuitively connected, and there are many ethical "gray areas" in business dealings.

Compliance Departments have typically been created by lawyers, human resources people, ethicists, academics, regulators, consultants, judges, and other non-business people. The departments are often the offspring of scandals, consent judgments, and Sarbanes-Oxley requirements. Compliance Departments are perceived as being imposed on business people as mandatory for some reason. It is not too presumptuous to believe that few business people developed the department's strategic directions or formulated some clear business-oriented objectives. Consequently, Compliance Departments are generally viewed as either the costs of penance or the price of continued virtue.

Compliance people have a tendency to side-step business realities. It's easier that way. Ethics is presented as a kind of moral absolutism. Examples in ethics training courses are often presented in a simplistic way, as if every real-life situation has a right and wrong answer (such as "should I lie, cheat and steal, or not"). With its emphasis on "doing the right thing," many managers believe that compliance people are simply asserting the obvious with no substantive guidance, so those managers do not take the message seriously. (Business people may also see no tangible benefit in "doing the right thing" if their compensation and financial targets focus only on results with no rewards for using only ethical tactics. The slogan then becomes empty sentiment.)

Third reality: Managers generally believe that investigations are neither profitable nor expeditious. Business people know that the profitable use of time is the key to their success, and the investigation may seem more expensive—in terms of time and money—than simply writing off the loss, firing the offending employee and going back to the business of selling profitable goods and services.

Fourth reality: Workplace investigations are usually not tied to the operation of the business. The preferred goals have been limited usually to identifying wrongdoers and calculating the harm they caused. The business people have already determined, for example, that Bob stole the money, so what does the investigation do for them?

Fifth reality: People who work in large companies learn that periodically, some new corporate fad pops up, and then everyone is supposed to pay homage to it. A succession of corporate slogans, mantras and "paradigm shifts" fosters in many colleagues either studied indifference or a this-too-shall-pass attitude. A Compliance Department that relies on abstract messages about ethics and compliance will eventually leave that department as just another layer of bureaucracy to be conveniently ignored and only mentioned periodically in superficial newsletters and lunchroom posters.

Increased attention to compliance and investigations will be considered a smart investment for your company's leadership if they believe that the risks of noncompliance are tangible. Otherwise, a greater emphasis on compliance and ethics becomes little more than an insurance policy—with its own share of overhead costs—for something that they perceive as not likely to happen.

This final point deserves some additional discussion. When calculating if and how to respond to business risks, smart executives focus both on the likelihood of something happening as well as the anticipated severity of that outcome if it were to occur. Credit checks for new customers and reserves for doubtful accounts, for example, reflect management planning for likelihood and severity. Although you will not have the data available to you that is similar to the data available to other departments, try to get as specific as possible regarding the risks your investigation efforts have identified. If you can discuss the likelihood and severity of additional incidents, even better.

Just remember that "otherwise something could happen" is not a very persuasive argument.

30) You need the company's leadership. They don't really need you.

Investigators are like dentists. People don't want to call on us, although they might be glad to know we're there just in case we are needed. And when they do need us, you will be able to fix the problem. It's only a question of how much it's going to hurt.

A common conceit among compliance people is a certainty that, for some reason, we are an intrinsic part of the company. It is difficult to see from where this assumption comes. Our contribution to the company is less tangible than, for example, the accounts-payable department, so we should be more focused on adding value than assuming it. Among compliance professionals, the challenge is greater for investigators because investigations can be outsourced to Human Resources, the Legal Department or a company vendor (although with less quality than we can deliver).

We need company managers as allies and advocates. An effective way to cultivate managers is to consider their needs and concerns in our strategic thinking. If necessary, ask them directly. Then include their needs and concerns in your investigation goals. Just because you are trying to determine what went wrong does not prevent you from similarly identifying what went right. Also, identifying where some business process needs to be improved does not require you to blame someone. Process gaps often arise because business processes are designed by honest people who limited their focus to whether the crafted process will be useful, efficient, and cost-effective. Opportunities for process improvement are frequently identified in misconduct investigations, not so much because of our crackerjack investigative skills, but because the business people did not "think like crooks" and foresee the possibility of employee wrongdoing. Investigators are professionally trained to think like dishonest people, and others generally are not.

You can influence how management values you. Critically ask yourself two questions: (1) are the investigators in your company aggressively taking a posture of finding misconduct (through training, awareness and referral-pipeline creation) rather than passively waiting for a report to arrive, and (2) are the issues being investigated consequential and meaningful to the profit-making goals of your company, or are they inconsequential in the scheme of the company's overall business interests? Everyone involved in your company's investigation process must answer these questions.

Work to change the answers if you are dissatisfied with them. Nothing stops you from exploring how to learn about misconduct proactively before an incident occurs. You have some control over whether you simply wait for the phone to ring.

As part of your investigative goals, are you regularly helping business people solve their business problems? If the wrongdoing affects a customer relationship, are you helping repair that relationship? If you make it a priority to stay business-focused and act as an advisor, the business people will become your allies. (And investigators need all the supporters we can get.)

The point here is that your company always has choices. Just because the company has to conduct some inquiry into possible misconduct does not mean it has to do it as effectively as you would like them to do it. The company can conduct bare-bones, check-off-the-box investigations if that is all the executives want. Or they could just outsource your function entirely. So never take your job security for granted. Always remind your executives through the quality of your efforts how smart they were to hire you.

31) Make sure you are in the right place in the company chart.

Don't assume that your company's leadership slotted your function in the most-effective place possible in the infrastructure. The department in which you reside and your reporting line may have less to do with effectiveness and more to do with historical accident.

Many Compliance Departments were established in the wake of a corporate scandal as a way to reassure investors, the marketplace and regulators. The structure, charter, reporting relationships and placement in the organization chart may have more to do with providing reassurance—not to mention someone's empire building—rather that functional effectiveness. Similarly, job descriptions for key compliance people may be overly broad template descriptions pulled from third-party sources and designed for external consumption rather than as a result of strategic planning for maximum effectiveness.

Regardless of what internal forces created your function, your place on the corporate totem pole today should be where you can approach investigations with independence and flexibility to make the maximum contribution to the business. In some companies, that means working as a staff function under the general counsel. In other companies, the function may report directly to the CEO outside the regular corporate structure so that decisions may be made without regard to the parochial needs of any particular business unit.

The key measurement is functional effectiveness. Some people may disagree and say objectivity and independence are paramount considerations. But they are wrong to limit the considerations only to the qualities of an impartial fact-finder. An investigator is a fact-finder, business advisor and fiduciary. You are genuinely effective when your place in the management structure helps fulfill each one of these responsibilities.

32) Management calculates the cost of responding to misconduct, so you should know the corresponding benefit.

You have completed your investigation and presented your findings. Naturally, after praising your excellent work, your company's managers swiftly apply your findings and correct the problems you so ably identified. Not always.

When confronted with proof of misconduct, management has two basic options: doing something or doing nothing. What are the costs of doing something versus doing nothing?

There are generally three areas to consider for the actions chosen by management to address a proven misconduct incident. These areas are psychological, social and financial.

The psychological cost of doing nothing will be the potential breakdown of management authority among employees who know both that misconduct occurred and that the company did nothing about it. The cost of doing something, however, will include embarrassment and the reaction of other employees when they learn what happened and the possible errors that inadvertently facilitated it.

The social costs of doing nothing are damage to the company's image and a negative influence on the workplace. The social costs of doing something are the disruption to the workplace and the negative publicity that comes from announcing that you have dishonest employees.

The financial costs of doing nothing are the future losses that may occur because this response creates a precedent and condones the acceptance of a loss. (Doing nothing tells other employees that it's okay to repeat the misconduct without consequences.) The cost of doing something is the expense involved, internally and externally, in redressing the misconduct. (And most of the costs, with a civil suit against someone with few assets for example, will never be recovered.)

Don't assume that, once you report your findings, management will leap to remedy what you uncovered. Some internal calculations are going to be made either way. And this reality dovetails with the earlier point about executives driving the bus. It's not your call, no matter how strongly you feel about the changes you believe are required.

33) Find the best way to measure internally the success of your workplace investigations process.

Some people believe a good measurement of compliance effectiveness is the number of hotline calls your company receives. This is the wrong measurement, because the success of the function should not depend on the willingness of a sufficiently aggrieved employee to pick up the phone.

Some people believe this measurement is the number of investigations opened. This is wrong, too, because this only looks at numbers and not the subject matter, seriousness nor time required to clear the case.

Some people believe the correct measurement is the subject matter because, after all, isn't an expense-account-padding case more important than an "I hate my boss" case? Not necessarily. The expense-account padder may be some guy who wants his meals paid for, while the other guy may be a boss who is so bad that the department of twenty is about to mutiny.

Simply put, the best way to measure your success internally is to hear it from your CEO, CFO and any other executive you consider to be a customer of your efforts. Let them tell you what's important. If it's important to them, you'll know it's a key factor to your professional success. Their feedback tells you directly whether your process is business-focused, has a good return on investment and is helping the company's bottom line. And if your process needs a realignment to match their priorities, you'll know exactly where to make the changes.

Because these are the people who also decide your compensation and job security, their perspectives are among the most important you can learn.

34) Know what your business leaders think about you and your process. Learn it from your biggest case.

Most workplace investigators will never be police detectives or work for a company that specializes in investigations. Instead, you most likely work in a corporate or academic setting, and your investigations work will be just one of the company's staff functions. When someone measures the value of your efforts, it will not be as simple as hours billed or revenue generated.

The challenge for an investigator—and probably for compliance professionals generally—is how you will prove your value. You face a number of obstacles. First, your leaders are not likely to be investigators, so they will not intuitively see, within the confines of your professional discipline, all that you are doing to protect the company and shareholder value. Second, even if they consider you and your function to be an asset to the company, by what criteria do they measure your value? (Do they even have some criteria other than some visceral appreciation for what you do?) Third, how difficult will it be for them to place a high value on you when you handle things they wished never happened in the first place?

A smart person tries to understand how his boss values his efforts. If we were salespeople, counting the number of deals closed or the revenue generated this calendar quarter would be easy. Make your numbers, and you're valued. Miss your target, and you're worthless to the company. (At least these colleagues get defined targets to meet. We usually don't enjoy the benefit of such clear expectations.)

Don't complacently accept your executives' statements of support at face value. Of course your company's leaders say they support your compliance efforts. How could they not? The alternative is to advocate non-compliance. But what do those statements of support realistically mean to your personal and professional goals? Do those words translate into something useful for you? They probably don't. (And, while we are on the topic, neither do the number of hotline calls, posters in the lunchroom nor the number of times they salute you with cafeteria cake on "Compliance Day.")

In the long run, you are better served by honest feedback and specific objectives rather than feel-good expressions of support which are, on a practical level, meaningless. How will that support focus your efforts on an area that concerns your executives? How will you be able in the future to point to a meaningful achievement if you aren't certain the bosses consider it meaningful?

The next challenge is that, for investigators at least, an abstract discussion of goals doesn't work so well when so much of our function is a reactive analysis. Most of our caseload—and therefore the value we contribute from it—comes to us from colleagues who report actual or suspected misconduct. Contrast that with ambitious sales people in your company who proactively search out fertile territory in which to sell your company's goods and services.

One solution is to use an investigation as a brief window of opportunity to know, at least on some level, precisely what they think about you and your process. While managers are considering the subject matter of your investigation and its possible fallout, you can perhaps see if they view you as an integral part of the risk-management team or just another layer of bureaucracy that has some operational claim on the allegation. You can hope they'll bombard you with questions, concerns and areas of inquiry to pursue. This shows you that they consider your fact-finding skills to be essential to solving their problems, rather than you being simply another corporate function running parallel to theirs. Listen to them carefully. When they tell you what is important to them, they have just told you how they intend to value your contribution to the collective problem.

The business leaders should support your efforts, but you need to recipro-cate—or take the initiative to cultivate—that support with business-focused investigations. Investigations offer a lot of professional and personal satis-faction. But professional and personal illusions are costly. Like most other relationships in your life, knowing where your truly stand is always best.

35) Know your customer.

Investigations are neither intellectual exercises nor steps on a journey toward some corporate ethical paradise. A good investigation specifically serves your company's business needs. Even though these people are your col-leagues, consider the term "customer" when you think about those who benefit from your efforts. Like any other service provider, our efforts are valuable if they are tailored to the needs those we intend our labors to serve.

This seems like a simple concept, but its application is not obvious. Your precise internal customer depends on the particular investigation. Some people may voluntarily seek your expertise, such as colleagues in Human Resources or the Legal Department, to investigate a specific allegation. These customers want help with a specific problem and seek a specialist to provide the fact-finding. But an internal customer may also be involved involuntarily in the investigations process, such as an implicated employee, reluctant wit-ness, or a manager who prefers to wish the problem away. Finally, a customer could be the company executives who rely on the investigation's findings to improve their business processes.

Simply put, your internal customer is the audience, recipient and ben-eficiary of your efforts. Identify the customer for each investigation you conduct. Your customer cannot just be some faceless corporate monolith. You'll get better results when you have someone specific in mind.

36) Serve your company well. The shareholders are paying for you too.

Everything in your company has to make business sense. Each department and function must generate revenue or reduce the risks of losing it. As you are currently doing it, does your job protect shareholder value? Can you explain the bottom-line significance of your job duties? Or do you see your value proposition as only removing wrongdoers from your midst.

Think big, be big. Think small, stay small. A company's injury from workplace misconduct—besides the immediate impact of the misconduct—often has additional consequences for the business, with a corresponding need for more information to help resolve those problems. For example, an internal company department may have become operationally dysfunctional because of the misconduct within it. Is this problem the result of multiple personality conflicts among department co-workers, weak management, a crushing workload, or a combination of all three? What is the precise dysfunction and how will it continue to affect the business? Similarly, a customer relationship may be threatened by employee misconduct, and the customer now seeks "assurances" (financial and otherwise) that it still has the right business partner. But what exactly happened—and didn't happen—and how should that knowledge be used so that the company does not over-respond to this customer demand for a handout? As another example, a misconduct incident may show that new internal procedures are needed to combat a problem that had hidden undetected until now. But how does the company respond to the precise business risk identified without smothering the sales department with another layer of internal bureaucracy?

Consider all the ways you can use the investigation to help the company. The failure to maximize the value of workplace investigations usually represents a failure of imagination about the benefit from an objective, credible analysis of the facts surrounding some incident or problem. The analysis, if expanded, can become the basis on which the relevant managers take needed corrective and preventive steps to protect all of the company's interests.

Every problem your company faces—sales, operations, accounting, legal, personnel, etc.—is a financial one, because the problem ultimately affects the bottom line. Investigating misconduct with only a focus on substantiating an allegation of misconduct against the implicated employee does little to protect the shareholders' investment if other problems remain unexplained. (In many cases, it's the other problems, like non-existent or malfunctioning processes, that pose the greater threat to shareholder value.) So focus your investigation goals on the bottom line. Make sure that you keep that business focus on the totality of business risks.

37) Fight the biases and preconceptions that are justifications NOT to do investigations.

If workplace investigations are perceived, however incorrectly, as punitive fact-finding expeditions, there will be a bias in your company against investigating, except in the rare instances where the initial facts appear so serious as to give management no alternative. But as a matter of company policy, there should be no justification not to do an investigation. If there is probable cause to believe that misconduct may have occurred, you cannot fairly ignore it and then claim to be acting in the best interest of the company.

You might encounter a particular manager who does not want an investigation to be conducted. This does not mean he is trying to hide something. Instead, his concern is likely about how the investigation would be conducted. Most likely, the concern can be traced back to past investigations conducted with a "we have to get to the bottom of this whatever the consequences" rather than a "let's figure out what happened so you can make some good business decisions when I am done" approach. So the bias against investigations is not necessarily one against investigations focused on helping the business.

Remember, the bosses don't need you if there aren't any—or enough—investigations. No one should try to investigate where it's not appropriate, because resources wasted on a trivial issue do more harm than good. But your bias should be towards encouraging as many investigations as possible.

38) Know your company's policies.

A purpose of every investigation is figuring out what happened and what didn't. Sometimes the substantiated misconduct is inherently wrong, like stealing or padding your expense account. Lawyers call this misconduct *malum in se* – wrong in and of itself.

But sometimes the misconduct is wrong only because your company decides it is wrong. For example, hiring your relatives may be forbidden by your company, or it may be allowed if certain conditions are met. Buying paper towels from your Uncle Ernie's company may be okay, for example, if you get multiple bids. It all depends.

So locate your company's human-resources and similar operating policies and keep them handy. These policies, along with your code of conduct, are the yardsticks by which your fact-finding should be measured to determine if misconduct occurred. (Company policies can be more helpful than the code of conduct, because the policies are usually very detailed about specific conduct that is either required or forbidden.) And if misconduct did occur, the extent of the policy deviation will guide management both to address the employee-specific issue as well as whether policy adjustments or additional training are needed.

39) Understand how your company's operations work.

Investigators are frequently called upon to make inquiries regarding how business is conducted in the various parts of the company. Besides investigating personal conduct alone—the executive who sexually harasses his secretary is a good example—you will more often investigate the conduct of an employee doing (or not doing) his job in a company department. If you work for a large company, it's easy to become overwhelmed or bewildered because you didn't know about, or had only cursory knowledge of, how the relevant department operates. However, substantive knowledge of the processes relevant to your investigation is crucial to any analysis of whether internal procedures were followed and, if not, why they weren't. Put simply, you cannot explain what happened unless you first understand what happened.

This is not to suggest that you should proactively study the operations of each internal department or try to become omniscient about your how your company works. The point is that, when the investigation begins, you should take some time to learn about the operations before you begin witness interviews. Investigation findings are helpful only if they are focused, precise, and substantive. General observations—assuming you're even competent to offer them—provide limited, if any, business value. You may end up doing nothing more than repeating what is already considered common knowledge.

A second reason for learning this information concerns witness credibility. You will not just be reviewing operations. You will also consider how the implicated person used—or misused—internal processes to commit misconduct. If the implicated person where trying to evade your detailed questioning about his adherence to a specific company policy, for example, knowing how the process works and the extent to which non-implicated people follow it is essential.

Take the time to learn about the normal business processes in the department. Figure out what normally happens. Review written procedures in order to have a basis for comparison. After that, if necessary, interview an uninvolved person in the department with personal knowledge of the process about which you care. Let that person help you understand what is important.

40) If investigations are handled by numerous departments, each department cannot investigate its own way.

In some companies, investigations are handled by a core group of people specialized to conduct them. In other companies, the responsibility is spread among numerous departments (Human Resources, Legal, Internal Audit, etc.), and the investigations are allocated according to the particular allegation. The challenge is to be sure all the investigations are conducted essentially the same way.

Inconsistencies among investigation techniques pose two specific risks. First, investigation processes in every company should be based on best practices (either for misconduct investigations generally or for your company's particular industry). So if some investigative approach is best for your company, is every investigator using it? And if they aren't, why not?

The second reason concerns process consistency. Without a standard approach, each investigator necessarily conducts his inquiries as he sees fit. (This is not to criticize a flexible approach that reflects an investigator's personal style in the needs of a particular case.) Without a protocol, you risk inconsistency in the investigations process. This variability might expose your company to a lawsuit by a terminated employee who wants to show that a similarly situated employee in another department was not terminated for the same offense.

Your company needs to have a formal investigations protocol. This establishes a baseline standard for everyone to follow. The standard protocol should include (1) how the reporter should be contacted, (2) how to determine the investigation plan; (3) how to inform management; (4) how to go about gathering documents; (5) how to conduct interviews; and (6) how to prepare investigation reports. This protocol needs to cover *how* the company wants each investigator to do his job.

All investigators must also be trained on basic interviewing and document-gathering techniques. Accumulated bad habits and multiple past investigations do not substitute for best-practices training. No matter how long the investigator has been working in his discipline, specialized training is important.

Third, investigations should be allocated according to the relative strengths of the department handling them. For example, human resources people spend their days dealing with people. An investigation whose success depends on the information learned through employee interviews is one to send to these professionals.

By contrast, a fraud case that requires careful study of internal financial documents might be assigned to your internal auditors because their jobs rely heavily on these reviews. Finally, an investigation that involves either a legal violation or poses a significant risk of litigation against the company might be conducted by your lawyers.

The point is that, despite common investigation steps, these professionals are not interchangeable. There is no generic investigation, and the assignment should be made after considering the needs of that case. Never assume that any one investigator can do every type of investigation with the same level of expertise.

41) Be proactive. Find something to do.

Misconduct is a normal characteristic of human behavior. Although the risk of misconduct can be reduced, it cannot be eliminated. Traditional approaches by Compliance Departments fail to appreciate that a company is always vulnerable to harm from employee misconduct. Similarly, when an investigation limits itself to the substance of the initial report, the investigator has unintentionally determined that the misconduct in the report is an aberration among the company's employees and operations. Because it is an aberration, there is no need to consider the possibility that the misconduct is occurring, or has the potential to recur, elsewhere in the company. It will remain unknown how many incidents of misconduct occur. Not because the incidents could not be prevented, but because the company did not earlier appreciate the vulnerabilities and gaps in its operations.

Consider the law-enforcement view of organized crime. An organized crime group exists solely to make money through criminal activities. Organized crime groups frequently infiltrate and attach themselves to legitimate businesses. The groups also create business entities through which crimes are committed. The group may conceal its activities within regular business operations or parasitically drain off legitimate company assets. These criminals are always searching for additional and better ways to enrich themselves.

Law-enforcement agencies appreciate this, so they often approach organized-crime investigations proactively. The proactive approach in this context means that police and prosecutors assume that organized crime is a constant risk (either to legitimate businesses or compliance with the law), and that organized crime perpetually looks for ways to make money. Consequently, law-enforcement agencies investigate organized crime by looking for the ways they are actively trying to make money illegally, such as a stock-trading boiler-room or a prepaid-telephone-card front company. The focus, by contrast, is not simply to investigate a police report made by a victimized business owner.

So how does this strategy apply to workplace investigations? Within any company, some employees will always be dishonest, and others may be dishonest under the right circumstances. Collectively, this means that, as with an organized crime group, there will always be employees committing misconduct. The risk to the company is always there. A proactive approach accepts this reality and uses the investigation process to identify company vulnerabilities and mitigate those risks. The initial report only provides the "window" into the company's operations to question where misconduct is occurring or may reasonably be expected to occur.

So don't just sit there and wait for a report to come to you. Talk to your company executives. Are there any operational risk areas about which they are concerned? Any problematic client relationships? Any dysfunctional departments where they know there is a problem but not what precisely the problem is? It's much easier to contribute value when the bosses tell you precisely where you should add it.

42) Don't call it a hotline.

Your company can give its reporting line any name it wants. But labels mean something. The chosen name communicates to your colleagues how the company anticipates its use and perceives its purpose.

Calling it a "hotline" might give your colleagues the impression that its only purpose is to receive calls from people who saw the CFO's secretary shred documents. Companies often compound the misconception when it is called a "whistleblower hotline." There are multiple definitions of a whistleblower. If this leaves ambiguity among compliance professionals, how perplexed is someone in another department going to be?

This labeling problem is another lost opportunity to portray the investigation process as a business function. The hotline label carries a bit of cachet, but why is it called a "hotline" anyway? We are company employees, not secret agents.

Sorry to take the excitement out of it, but the phone number is just a reporting line. It is just one way to learn of reports. It exists to allow people to report concerns anonymously and/or outside their management chains. There really is no need for a buzzword, especially one that leads people to think that management is not concerned about anything other than sink-the-company allegations of financial misconduct.

43) Figure out ways to get people to make more hotline reports.

Originally, the intended purposes of a compliance hotline were either to facilitate the reports of people shredding financial documents at 2 a.m., or to learn about colleagues who did not treat each other with the "mutual respect"—whatever that really means—as most company codes of conduct generally require. Hotlines have evolved into a reporting mechanism for an employee who wants to make a report outside of his management structure and possibly do it anonymously.

Although the purposes of hotlines have changed, and despite the effects of establishing codes of conduct, low usage is still a problem. There remains both a taboo against reporting misconduct as well as a concern that anonymous reporters will be identified (despite the company's promises to the contrary). The precise reasons for low reporting will be different for each company. If your company has a low reporting rate, learn why more people don't report their concerns. (When you encounter it in your interviews, invest in a few additional witness questions to find out.)

You probably understand your company, its history and its culture. Is the issue just a lack of awareness, so that employees would ring the hotline off the wall if only they knew what number to call? Is it a fear that the implicated people will find out who made the report and seek retaliation? Or is it simply cynicism that, even if reported, the company will do nothing about it? Each of these is a different problem that leads to a different solution. The solution in your company, however, is not more posters, wallet cards or cafeteria cake for "Compliance Day."

Some companies have a mandatory reporting policy to encourage employee reporting of actual or suspected misconduct. Under this policy, each employee, as a condition of employment, is required to report suspected or actual misconduct. An employee can be disciplined for failing to report it. The rationale is that each employee is a company fiduciary, so he must alert management when he believes misconduct may be happening. Otherwise, an employee is entitled to collect a paycheck while standing idly by watching the company suffer harm.

The employee may make the report to his manager, to another internal department (like Human Resources) or to the hotline. The reporter may remain anonymous if he prefers. But a report must be made.

Another step is to ask management to make an appropriate announcement when an employee who stepped forward led to an investigation that actually helped the company stop misconduct. Conversely, if someone is terminated for retaliating against a reporter, witness or other person in your investigation, make sure others know that the company means what it says when it has a zero-tolerance policy.

Finally, encourage your company's leadership to publicize investigation outcomes that, even if the facts are well-scrubbed, show that the system works and management cares. The best executives will see the investigation process as a matter of "corporate hygiene" rather than simply airing the company's dirty linen.

44) Make friends. Don't just wait for the phone to ring.

Your effectiveness depends on learning of misconduct allegations when they arise in your company. Whether that information comes to you through the hotline or through some other internal source does not matter.

If you only wait for the hotline to ring, you have staked your job security on whether a co-worker feels sufficiently aggrieved to pick up the phone and voluntarily report something.

Polish your diplomatic skills and make strong alliances with your colleagues in Human Resources, the Legal Department, and the CFO's company. When problems arise—and these are problems more significant than the "I hate my boss" variety—you will be among the first to know. Please remember that you depend on them for your job effectiveness. These departments likely prospered without you long before there were Compliance Departments. Your company clearly didn't collapse under the weight of all that uninvestigated misconduct.

This is not a turf issue. Their role is different than yours, and you have expertise in investigations. They usually don't, or their investigation abilities are rudimentary. The converse is also true. You should not be handling traditional human resources cases, even if they come through the hotline. By focusing on which skill set and job function serves that particular need, rather than fighting over turf, you can make it work.

45) Few hotline calls are not a good thing.

If your company gets only a handful of hotline calls, consider what that means. If you have a number of internal "pipelines" to learn about possible misconduct when it occurs—for example, referral criteria with Human Resources, the Legal Department and the CFO organization, than the number of hotline calls is not critical. If you rely almost exclusively on the hotline for your caseload, you may be in trouble.

You are a company investigator. If there is possible or actual misconduct, you should want to learn of it regardless of the way that information reaches you. Reports may come from Human Resources, the CFO's office, the Legal Department, or some other department that learns about these things. Your hotline should be considered as just another internal-reporting mechanism that allows people to make reports outside the normal management structure and anonymously if they wish.

The hotline should also be the final option promoted by your company. It should be the last resort of a person who wants to be anonymous or does not want—either through fear or concern that it will be ignored—to report it through his management or another department.

Regardless of how the report gets made, make sure your company's infrastructure directs it to you. When someone asks you whether you investigate the misconduct in your company, answering "just the ones they tell me about" is not a career-enhancing response.

46) Two secret reasons for a code of conduct.

Many people believe that codes of conduct lead to ethical employee behavior. Few statistics, however, show that these companies are any more ethical than companies without them. Codes of conduct are ubiquitous, but the fact that they are commonplace may have more to do with a company's desire to appear responsible in the marketplace rather than anything else. (If this sounds too cynical, then why hasn't the number of misconduct cases investigated reduced as a result of code proliferation?) Window-dressing and posturing have their places, but the code alone is not a behavior modifier.

Companies establish a code of conduct for two important reasons. Neither has anything to do with fostering ethical behavior. First, a code allows the company to set down its fundamental rules for employee behavior. The existence of the code allows the company to enforce its requirements against those employees who violate its provisions. That's not a bad thing for investigators because it gives us a benchmark to measure the employee behavior we investigate.

A code of conduct also scores points in litigation and with regulators because it shows that the company proactively specified employee conduct standards. The company can then try to prove that a sexually harassing boss, for example, represents an aberration rather than someone who was acting under the company's indifference to improper conduct.

The second reason for a code of conduct is to remove the taboo against using the company's ethics hotline. This taboo is commonplace. Most of us were raised not to tell on people and to mind our own business. Being called a tattletale was never a compliment. So a company needs to make reporting concerns socially acceptable among its employees in order to neutralize the forces against reporting. Promoting the hotline makes reporting suspicions of possible misconduct the laudable act of good corporate citizenship by an employee who understands his fiduciary duty to the company.

As a final and related thought, understand how your executives view the hotline. Promoting its availability is something every company does, but do your executives actually care if someone calls? You'll have little to investigate if the hotline stays unused. Your ability to make an important contribution depends on its robust use by your colleagues. Be sure the executives follow through beyond just announcing the hotline is available, in case some sufficiently aggrieved employee feels sufficiently motivated to use it.

47) Don't let them hyperventilate. Control the initial impact of the allegation.

Most of the time, a report of possible or actual misconduct will be received confidentially and quietly. This gives you plenty of time to make your initial inquiries discreetly and with minimal disruption to the business. The reporter can be interviewed, the potential issues clarified, and the investigation steps determined. You get to approach the matter in the ordinary course of business and schedule interviews and travel as you integrate the case into your existing caseload.

But sometimes the initial report comes in with a big flourish and some urgency. A potential scandal with internal and external consequences is brewing. Your company's rumor, gossip and damage-control operations are ramping up. Urban legend and rank speculation abound about what people are certain happened. People seem to have jumped to conclusions even before you've asked your first question.

The first task in your new case is to slow—and calm—everyone down. Spreading hysteria is always more entertaining than dealing with facts. Although there are exceptions, most initially sensational reports actually have mundane root causes like incompetence, process failures, lax management, and poor perception management.

All this tumult presents you with an opportunity. Use the chaos as your opportunity to exert your control over the fact-finding process and to secure your place at the management table. (At the risk of sounding cynical, it may be one of the few times executives return your calls promptly and have sufficient schedule flexibility to meet with you regularly.) Be responsive to competing concerns of managers, department heads, and executives, but don't neglect both your role and obligations to both the company and the investigation.

Everyone needs to approach the issue calmly and realistically and let you do your job. Investigating misconduct in an environment like this can be difficult with emotions and speculation running high. By bringing the collective temperature down, you can manage expectations by focusing the executives on business priorities, not just sensational speculation.

By the way, you have no reason to hyperventilate either. Keep a sense of proportionality with the investigation as well. You will encounter few cases where you may legitimately ignore the fact that you operate with limited resources.

48) Manage the expectations of managers so you can fight premature conclusions before establishing actual facts.

The expectations of senior management must be carefully managed. They should be advised to wait until all the facts are in. They should be reminded that premature conclusions hurt the business because they would be making decisions on incomplete information. However, if they show a tendency over time to reach premature conclusions, consider whether you may be at least partially responsible if your investigations are not being completed in a timely way and efficiently (according to their needs, not just your own timetable for clearing cases).

It is human nature to reach conclusions based on hunches and past experience. But don't let your colleagues derail the quality of your investigation—which is based on objective facts—by their impatience.

Executives want investigations completed quickly for valid reasons. No one should expect them to wait forever, but don't sacrifice completeness for expediency. Also accept that there might be some friction because executives are used to controlling events in your company. An investigation is one place they cannot do so, although they remain concerned about the outcome.

Solicit their views, and respond to their concerns. You may learn that they need to advise the Board of Directors or outside auditors. They may worry how to explain things to the media and key clients.

Most importantly, keep them informed of your progress, tentative findings, open issues and potential problems. Don't be mysterious or take a leave-it-all-to-me attitude. They are your business partners, and often their needs are very real. Keep them in the loop as you investigate. Manage their expectations and keep your investigation business- focused.

Close collaboration also gives you the chance to showcase both your expertise and value to the company as an in-house resource. You might accomplish more in one significant investigation to demonstrate your value than in all the posters, codes and Compliance Day cake you've peddled until then.

49) Retaliation is based far more on perception than reality.

Investigators are not naïve people (or at least the good ones aren't). After enough experience, we learn not to make rosy assumptions about the content of another person's character. It is easy to think—a common occurrence among reporters and witnesses—that once the implicated person learns of the information you were given, it's payback time for the witness. But this is rarely the case. People implicated in misconduct are more likely to go into damage-control mode to save their jobs rather than affirmatively seek out the people who cooperated with you. Most colleagues in trouble are more concerned with self-preservation than handing management an easy reason to fire them.

Investigators cannot singularly establish employee trust in a workplace where they believe retaliation is alive and well. A good investigation will not only deal with retaliation concerns when they arise but will also try to preempt them in the first place.

This tactic is more than just process fairness. If retaliation concerns pervade your company, many people will be discouraged from making reports or cooperating fully with your inquiries. These are two things you can't afford to let happen.

Every company must have a zero-tolerance policy against retaliation. This policy is usually part-and-parcel with the creation of a hotline, code of conduct, and ethics policy for senior managers. The existence of a policy in your company, however, should not persuade you that it will discourage the conduct it prohibits. (A retaliating employee is motivated by fear or revenge. His decision-making is colored by those emotions and is not likely susceptible to considerations of a company policy.) Instead, the policy's value lies in the fact that violating it is grounds for immediate dismissal.

When retaliation concerns arise, the issue is usually the perception of retaliation, not the real thing. The investigation may make people standoffish or withdrawn, for example, leading others to infer that some kind of payback has occurred. The foundation for the perception usually comes from a fear of the consequences of making the initial report or assisting the investigation. This fear probably results from past instances where finger-pointing was more important than identifying areas for business improvement. Whatever its causes, the problem is yours, although you did nothing to create it. Use the investigation process to show that the company cares more about corrective business problems with a financial impact rather than looking for heads to roll.

But also accept that the perception will be there.

PART III

Protect Your Case: How To Conduct An Effective Workplace Investigation

The most important part of the process, of course, is the investigation itself. A quality investigation brings value to the company and assists the business managers who must correct the situation you have investigated. A workplace investigation also tangibly affects the people involved, from the implicated employee who may be terminated to the manager who may be blamed for what he did or didn't do, or should have done.

A good investigator never forgets that real-world consequences are the results of his efforts. This outcome is different from that of other departments in the company. For instance, the accounts-receivable people can assume a certain percentage of bad debts from customers no matter how diligent their efforts, or the sales people can know that a significant amount of time and resources will be spent on potential customers who never wind up buying anything. We are only human, and we are not infallible. But we must remember that our colleagues will pay personally for our sloppiness and mistakes. "Good enough" should never be good enough for us.

50) It's not what you know. It's what you can prove.

Although investigators tend to—or at least should—have specialized training, don't underestimate the value of your own common sense. Many times your common sense will spell out for you what likely happened or didn't happen in the events under investigation.

But common sense can have its limits in your fact finding. For example, you are just so sure that Bob falsified his expense account. You are certain of his motive, his opportunity and his narcissistic view that the company does not appreciate him. But despite your gut feelings, you cannot find enough proof that the expenses he submitted for reimbursement had no business purpose. Bob has also denied everything. So what can you do?

Essentially you are stuck. A fundamental rule of the courtroom is that the burden of proof is on the prosecution to prove the allegations. This rule applies to workplace investigations too. Hunches, even your own moral certainty, don't count. All that counts is the relevant, valid proof you gathered. Your gut feeling is no substitute for evidence. You either get enough proof, or the implicated person is off the hook, at least until some future time when new information comes to light.

51) You have flexibility with the investigation, if you can defend it.

Investigators are generally free to select what seem to be the most effective methods of collecting, analyzing, and recording all relevant information. You may use any lawful method you think is most effective to complete your fact finding.

If your company has an investigation protocol, follow it. But remember that the protocol is not a straightjacket. It is only a default set of investigation standards your company wants you to follow. Deviations are expected when a particular investigation requires.

Be prepared, however, to defend any deviation from the protocol. Any deviation must be an informed decision that will, it is hoped, result in a better investigation result for the company, and a result that remains fundamentally fair to the employees involved. Sooner or later, you'll have to explain your decisions in a particular investigation and justify them.

52) Substance beats process every time.

Compliance-process owners regularly compile data on workplace investigations. Trends are examined, and problematic business processes are identified. The data is often shared with colleagues in other departments, often at quarterly meetings, where everyone reviews the same pie charts, pulls their chins in concentration, and agrees that the company should now do something different because of these insights. Then, typically, nothing happens, and another meeting is held in three months. In other words, people have just acquired the investigator's work, massaged it, and then presented it as their own insights.

The investigation process is where the facts are learned. The investigation process validates whether your company's training is effective and whether people trust your hotline. Workplace investigations are an important way to show whether the compliance program adds shareholder value—by increasing revenue or reducing unacceptable business risk—or whether the program is unfortunately just feel-good window-dressing.

The bottom line: there is a time for analysis, and there is a time for the brass-tacks work of an internal investigation. Each is useful, but the two are not interchangeable. Don't fall into the trap of believing that massaging information learned through the efforts of others is the same as doing the necessary, and sometimes unpleasant, work of gathering that information.

Be the one who adds substance and contributes value. Leave the arm-chair analysis to others.

53) If it does not happen at work, you don't care.

Some misconduct allegations involve sensitive issues. For example, the executive who everyone believes is having a romantic relationship with his assistant, or the sexually harassing manager who others tell you has just filed for divorce. As you investigate issues of personal conduct, you might be tempted to consider their alleged actions in the greater context of that person's life, not just their work. After all, when a witness volunteers that your implicated person is generally known to have a failed marriage, isn't that relevant to establishing a motive behind his flirting with every woman in the office?

Employees are entitled to their privacy, however. An employer may only invade that privacy to the extent the employer has to make necessary inquiries. So, unless an employee's conduct occurs either at work or somehow within the context of his employment, you have no right to ask about it. To do so is not only irrelevant—you are investigating workplace misconduct—but you might expose the company to an invasion-of-privacy claim (at the minimum).

You can often preempt this risk. At the beginning of each investigation, inform the witness—both the implicated person and anyone else who may know of the witness's personal life—that you only seek information on work-related behavior. Explain that you do not wish to know more than that.

When you "inoculate" the witness not to give you more than a limited answer, you protect yourself and the company. If the witness volunteers the information, you may accept it (although you should write in your notes that the witness volunteered it). But even if it's volunteered, consider if for background information only. The information may give you some insights or point you to areas of relevant permissible information, but non-office topics are usually of limited value when trying to prove workplace misconduct.

54) The office extends farther than the office.

You should investigate misconduct wherever it arises in the employment context. This extends beyond company offices and worksites. Conduct which occurs on a company-sponsored outing, training meeting, or other sanctioned off-premises event is subject to the same rules—and the company is subject to the same liability—as if it happened in the company's office.

Some employees do crazy things when on business trips or at company conventions. Their behavior is subject to the same scrutiny as if it were occurring on their work desk rather than in a hotel room. The company risks liability and harm from this behavior just the same as if it occurred down the hall from the CEO's office.

55) No fishing expeditions asking unrelated people on background in search of an issue.

Sometimes in the search for probable cause and usually before you are brought into the loop, managers many contact some trusted colleagues for their views as to whether the implicated person might be capable of the complained-about conduct. These managers aren't trying to defame anyone as much as understand the dimensions of the problem they have just encountered. In fact, these managers would probably defend their inquiries as an appropriate way to understand what may have happened.

There are times when appropriate inquiries could be made regarding what the person contacted heard in the past about the conduct under investigation. But these are inquiries you should make, if needed, in the initial phase of your investigation. Whoever asks the question, the views of those colleagues should never be solicited to determine if the reported activity sounds like the kind of thing the implicated person might have done. This communication is potentially defamatory. It is also useless to the investigation.

What matters to you is what the implicated person did and whether you can prove it. It is of little help that uninvolved people who were contacted believe that the implicated person might be the kind of person to do that sort of thing. That is speculation, not probable cause or relevant information.

56) Unless you have probable cause, leave your employees alone.

Generally speaking, employees have the right to be left alone to do their jobs. Even though an investigation may be needed from time to time, an investigation should never be a "fishing expedition" in order to locate some elusive misconduct believed to be lurking around your company.

Your company's leadership has given you limited corporate authority. You cannot open an investigation indiscriminately. Similarly, a reporter does not have the right to insist on an investigation simply because your company has an investigation function or promotes its hotline. An investigation is appropriate—and your authority kicks in—only if the initial report gives you probable cause to believe that misconduct has occurred. Never make any promises or commitments that action will be taken, other than that the information will be looked into.

What is probable cause? Probable cause is a criminal-justice concept. It reflects the value judgment that people are entitled to be free from scrutiny unless some basic factual threshold is satisfied. Probable cause means (1) that you reasonably believe a violation of your code of conduct, law or regulation may have occurred in your workplace, and (2) you reasonably believe that the named employee committed it. If you have probable cause, an investigation is now proper. Otherwise, an investigation is not appropriate at that time. (However, if later facts establish the probable cause, than an investigation should be opened.)

57) Words have meaning.

Workplace investigations are similar to their criminal-justice counterparts. And because proven misconduct may sometimes actually be criminal—for example, colluding with an outside vendor to approve phony invoices and then splitting the money—the temptation exists to adopt the law-enforcement nomenclature. Resist the temptation, however.

Ours is a business function, even if it is not always easy to show it. If we adopt words which are imprecise or freighted with meaning from another context, we will obscure our business purpose. We cannot fight all the stereotypes or preconceived notions, but we can set the right example with a careful selection of terms that reinforce our business purpose:

- **Report**. This is the information presented by a colleague or third party, which is intended to identify possible or actual misconduct by a company employee. It is not an "allegation" or similar term because you haven't yet verified the information to determine whether probable cause exists to warrant an investigation. The information in the report may lack credibility, it may be fabricated, or it may identify conduct that is not improper. At best, the information in the report is just a starting point for your inquiries.
- **Implicated person**. This is the person who may have committed misconduct. The terms "suspect" or "target" are not appropriate. He is not a criminal. The person you are investigating is still your colleague. Even if substantiated, the misconduct will likely be only a violation of your company's internal rules.
- **Substantiated**. This means only that you assembled sufficient proof to show that the misconduct more likely than not occurred. Using "guilty" or words that indicate conclusively

that the misconduct occurred is discouraged. The former is a poor choice because there has not been a trial. The latter is a poor choice because you don't know for certain that the misconduct occurred. You only know that sufficient information shows that it more likely than not that the misconduct happened.

- **Unsubstantiated**. Conversely, this does not mean that the implicated person is innocent. It only means that you were unable to assemble sufficient proof to show that the misconduct likely occurred. Your colleague may actually have committed the misconduct.

- **Inconclusive**. This means that, despite your efforts, you could not access enough information to determine whether or not the allegation could be substantiated. It is not the same as unsubstantiated because unsubstantiated presumes that you had access to all the documents and witnesses reasonably needed to make a full inquiry. A good example of an "inconclusive" finding is where essential witnesses have since left the company and refuse to be interviewed now, or where needed documents have been lost or destroyed.

- **Unfounded**: This means that there was insufficient information to give you probable cause and warrant an investigation. This is not the same as unsubstantiated, because here you did not begin gathering proof of whether misconduct occurred. An "unfounded" determination is appropriate where the initial report complained about conduct that was not misconduct even if you assumed the reporter's facts were accurate. A good example is where the complained-about conduct was within the boundaries of a manager's reasonable discretion.

- **Resolved**. This term means that you handled an inquiry or assisted with the resolution of an issue, but you did not conduct an investigation. Making inquiries to assist the company's lawyers render legal advice to the company and then completing that effort is a good example.

Besides choosing the right words, don't sprinkle your writings with corporate-speak or words with unnecessary complexity. So skip the "paradigm shift" and "thinking outside the box." And if Bob punched Steve in the parking lot, say just that instead of explaining how "the witness observed an assault and battery." Just say what you mean clearly and simply. Let the results of your efforts shine through.

58) Keep things confidential while disclosing on a need-to-know basis.

The importance of keeping all investigation-related information confidential cannot be overemphasized. Maintaining confidentiality is critical to the integrity of your investigation. If you don't ensure strict confidentiality throughout the investigation, your failure may have serious consequences:

- Someone's reputation may be damaged if others learn of the report, even if the allegation is found to be unfounded.
- The success of the investigation can be undermined if others know you are conducting one.
- The implicated person might engage in cover-up activities when he learns that he is being investigated.
- The company might be vulnerable to negative publicity or liability.
- The company's ability to defend any legal action associated with the matter may be damaged.
- The disclosure of information (or misinformation) may cause retaliation or witness intimidation.

All fine and good, but it does create a bit of a dilemma. Investigations are a business process, not a secret search for wrongdoing. They also tend to disrupt operations, despite your efforts to minimize the disruption. Business managers need to know what you are investigating, and how things are proceeding. If interim steps are needed, such as sending the implicated person home on full pay, you will have to tell the managers something. "Just trust me" is not a sufficient, professional response to a manager's request for a status report or information to justify the interim steps.

You have a qualified privilege to disclose information on a need-to-know basis. This basis comes in two parts: (1) does this person need to know something about the investigation at this moment, and (2) what precisely does this person need to know? If you can sufficiently answer these questions, go ahead. This is a topic where the "you're damn right I did" standard will serve you well. Just remember to limit the information to what that person needs.

Don't pretend that even the existence of an allegation won't affect the implicated person's reputation. You have an obligation to do all you can reasonably do to protect the reputations of all concerned and the company's interests as well.

Excessive disclosures of information pose some risks. First, the person you discuss may claim defamation, damage to his career prospects, or some other real or imagined grievance. (What better way to get some insurance against the fallout from a substantiated misconduct finding?) Second, excessive disclosure undermines your investigation either by tipping off witnesses to the specific issues you find important, or the disclosures may chill future testimony by witnesses who—justifiably or not—fear you will blab their personal details too.

The need for confidentiality begins when the initial report is received, but it does not end with the conclusion of the investigation. The fact that an investigation is underway or is being considered, the subject matter of it, the process followed, the materials or information gathered and the results of the investigation must always be treated confidentially. This protection includes being careful before using the details of an investigation at some later point in time.

On a related note, never promise complete or absolute confidentiality to a witness, reporter or anyone else. There is no way to guarantee it in all circumstances. (Once again, never say always, and never say never.)

59) Know your burden of proof.

To be fair to the employees implicated in your investigation, you have a burden of proof to satisfy. This means that you have to gather evidence to substantiate each element of the misconduct allegedly committed.

Once the proof is gathered, it has to be measured against a standard of proof. This is whether you have gathered enough proof to consider the allegation to be substantiated.

The applicable standard of proof in a workplace investigation is a "preponderance of the evidence." An allegation is considered proven if, based on the facts learned and the documents reviewed, it is more likely than not—think 51 percent or more—that the misconduct actually happened. If so, the allegation is considered substantiated. If not, the allegation is considered unsubstantiated.

The preponderance-of-the-evidence standard is not a criminal-justice standard. The criminal-justice standard is "beyond a reasonable doubt." This means that the proof makes it at least 90 percent certain that the misconduct actually happened. This difference in standards is another reason why the right to remain silent and the right to a lawyer—both constitutional rights in criminal cases—don't apply to employees in workplace investigations.

This topic underscores why you should avoid criminal-justice concepts and standards in your investigations. For example, if you adopted the beyond-a-reasonable-doubt standard, this would force you, among other things, to spend more resources and time than needed. It would also result in substantiated misconduct going unpunished when you cannot meet a 90 percent standard, although you may have satisfied the 51 percent standard that did apply.

60) Corroborate material facts.

Even with different standards of proof, workplace investigations continue to bear some resemblance to their criminal-justice counterparts. In a criminal case, a defendant's confession is not enough to justify the acceptance of a guilty plea. The police must also produce evidence to corroborate the material facts of the confession to show that it is accurate. (Judges are wary of accepting false confessions.)

This is also true in our world. If you are investigating a theft case, it is not enough to sustain the allegation against Bob simply because he admits taking a laptop from the office that was not assigned to him. However, if in speaking to Mary, she checks the serial number of the laptop and confirms that it was assigned to someone else who did not give Bob permission, then you have corroboration of the material facts to support Bob's admission.

The point here is that the material facts in your investigation need to be supported by a second source. The second source could be a witness or a document. The important part is that the existence of the fact to your findings does not depend on only one source. It's better to have the fact bolstered by something else to support its accuracy and reliability.

61) The investigation objective is decided up front. It is refined as you go.

Too many investigations begin either as a mad scramble to learn every possible fact or with a lackadaisical approach that usually means the investigator is gathering evidence in search of an allegation. Either way, the investigation becomes inefficient, sloppy, and disruptive and generally wastes limited resources. The investigation result will also be poor and unfocused.

These problems usually indicate that an investigation objective has not been specified. An investigation objective is nothing more than the answer to a simple question: what does the investigation need to prove? You can investigate more efficiently and effectively if you identify from the outset the precise allegation you intend to investigate.

This determination doesn't sound especially profound, but it's a simple step that's frequently overlooked. Grab a cup of coffee, and spend a few moments thinking about the information you have so far. Does it look like employee misconduct or a possible crime? Does it look like a specific company policy was violated, or is it some more generic misconduct like poor management supervision? Does it appear that only a rogue employee is involved, or could it be a perfect storm of unacceptable factors, which conspired to create the problem?

Once you've finished your coffee and answered these questions (at least for now), you should then identify the component elements of the alleged wrong. From that point, you determine the information you will need and how you will get it.

An investigation strategy is not engraved in stone. The initial investigation strategy might change as the investigation proceeds. Changing the strategy as the investigation proceeds and additional information is learned is actually a good thing. It shows you are testing your assumptions and proofs against the facts as you are learning them. When needed, you are adjusting your approach. This ensures that your investigation results will be supported by the proof you assembled.

62) We don't plan to fail. We fail to plan.

Every investigation requires you to do some thinking and analysis. You can ensure a good result by doing as much up-front thinking as possible. Once you have identified your investigation objective, the next step is to make an investigation plan.

The detail required, and the time consumed, to plan an investigation depends on the complexity of the allegation. Routine investigations usually require minimal time and detail, and a simple outline or summary may be sufficient. Complex investigations need more time and require finely developed planning.

Your investigative plan is simply the outline of how you intend to conduct the fact-finding process so you can obtain the facts necessary to prove the elements of the allegation. The plan serves as a checklist to ensure all necessary points are covered thoroughly and efficiently. Although created at the start of an investigation, a plan should be updated continually, not only to document the steps you've already completed, but also to reflect the changes—in objective, allegations, strategy, lines of inquiry, additional concerns, etc.—that become necessary as the evidence is developed.

There is another benefit of doing your thinking up front. A well-considered investigative plan that is conscientiously updated later becomes the outline for your investigative report. This makes report drafting more efficient. It also ensures a logical consistency and progression from allegations to fact finding to fact presentation. Once the framework is constructed, you only need to fill in the facts.

Part of the planning includes determining the scope of the investigation. The scope is different than the objective, but it is part of the same continuum. The objective is the ultimate purpose of the investigation, such as whether Bob defrauded the company by colluding with an outside consultant to submit fictitious invoices. The scope looks at the fact parameters needed to substantiate the allegation. Continuing with Bob, the scope would include analyses of the invoice-review and accounts-payable procedures. But the scope would not include inquiries into Bob's marriage or private life.

Defining the scope is fact-intensive. Simply put, what facts are you trying to learn? Is the allegation related to a company policy only? If so, then the investigation would focus on the relevant facts, comparing that to the specified company policy, and then suggesting remedial action. If the investigation concerns criminal conduct or financial irregularities, then the investigation may also assess possible criminal and civil exposure for the company and the individuals involved.

A proper investigation scope reinforces the fairness of the process. If the company must later defend a decision based on the investigation—a wrongful termination claim, for example—it will appear unreasonable for an employer to have reached a conclusion based on no or scattered evidence, or no real investigation at all. Also, it will appear unfair if the company disciplines an employee based on weak evidence when better or stronger evidence was reasonably available but ignored.

Proper definition of the scope also protects the innocent. A properly conducted investigation will identify any wrongdoers, but that does not mean that other individuals might not be injured as a result of the fact-finding. The importance of defining the scope of an investigation is, in some ways, an effort to protect the innocent, to narrowly define the fact-finding area to be investigated, and to assure that those not involved in a particular act of misconduct are neither implicated by their proximity to the event nor exonerated by omission.

There are serious consequences if the investigation scope is too narrow or too broad. You need to get to the root cause of the problem and not just deal with its symptoms. If your investigation is superficial, an underlying business problem will not be addressed, and the workplace will be exposed to further disruption. However, an overly broad investigation can equally harm the workplace culture and disrupt the business.

The scope can change anytime you believe there is actually more or less misconduct than originally thought. If you change the investigation scope (and the plan), simply add a contemporaneous note to the file documenting the new scope and your reasons for changing it. This could help you later on if you are accused of having some improper motive when you adjusted the investigation scope.

Once the scope has been determined, you can move to the next part of the plan: the strategy. A proper strategy, regardless of the investigation's complexity, makes the investigation process thorough and professional. The strategy is also the next stop on the checklist after objective and scope.

The scope gave you the fact parameters, which only constitutes a broad outline of your fact inquiry. The strategy takes it a step further and looks at the important granular issues, such as which people do you need to interview, and what documents do you need to review. The objective and scope determinations were critical to focusing your inquiry, but they neither give you any proof nor direct you to a promising source of relevant information.

The quality of your fact-finding depends significantly on your strategy. Who can give you the relevant information you need to substantiate each element? What documents should you seek? Do you need expense reports or access to the computer server to review someone's emails? If you estimate your needs too narrowly, you might miss someone or something. But if you estimate too broadly, you may overlook something important while wading through a morass of marginally relevant information. So, although a strategy should be adjusted as the investigation proceeds and you learn more, try to get it right the first time. This way, any adjustments are merely refinements and fine-tuning rather than wholesale changes that force you to retrace earlier steps.

As the investigation proceeds, stay flexible. Situations change, and you will want to adapt. The true nature of the problem under investigation may turn out to be different from what you first thought. Similarly, the witness list should be a "running" list, because different or additional witnesses may surface during the investigation. Do not let the investigation plan become so rigid that you can't alter it when necessary.

Keep in mind, however, that although you are an objective fact-finder, you are not neutral. Your role is more like a prosecutor's, and your investigation plan should reflect that. You are interested in proving that misconduct occurred if you can gather enough proof. You aren't indifferent to whether or not you can prove it. Like a prosecutor, however, you are interested in justice if the facts show that that implicated person is, in fact, innocent.

63) What didn't happen is as important as what did.

People love to jump to conclusions, especially during investigations. Speculating can be enjoyable water-cooler chitchat, and it tends to be more exciting than the mundane truth. Most misconduct is more often the result of poor and/or irresponsible decisions than intentionally wrongful behavior. Managers often view the allegation in the most-sinister light, and this can lead to a harmful overreaction, both in terms of personnel decisions as well as process changes.

Your investigation findings must tell a story. Of course, this means explaining what happened. But to ensure that management responds appropriately, it is sometimes necessary to explain what didn't happen. This allows the scrutinized conduct to be placed in context. So make sure you can offer this perspective and plan to write a full narrative when you are done. Tell the whole story.

An overreaction by management to an allegation of misconduct may be worse than an under-reaction. And it doesn't help the business either way.

64) If you want to substantiate a crime (or its workplace version) you have to prove each element.

It is never enough to make an investigation finding of "Bob stole the money." Your investigation requires a more precise finding if you want to contribute any value to the company. You must satisfy the burden of proof for each element of the offense.

One again, there is a parallel here to criminal justice. For example, to convict a defendant of criminal fraud, a prosecutor must prove—beyond a reasonable doubt—each of the elements: (1) a misrepresentation to the company of a material fact; (2) that was known to be false when said; (3) that was intended to cause the company to rely on it; (4) the company relied on it; and (5) the company suffered damages as a result. The prosecution has to develop sufficient facts to substantiate each element by the requisite standard of proof. Each element must be proven. If even one element cannot be proven—assume there were insufficient evidence of whether the misrepresented fact was "material"—the defendant goes free. In other words, the prosecutor is assembling evidence not to prove "fraud," but to prove each of five requisite elements.

The same approach applies to workplace investigations. Consider your company policy on sexual harassment. It probably defines sexual harassment as: (1) intentional, unwanted discrimination based on sex, (2) the harassment was severe or pervasive, (3) the harassment negatively affected the work environment, (4) the harassment would detrimentally affect a reasonable person of the same sex, and (5) management knew or should have known of the harassment, and did nothing to stop it.

Focusing on the requisite elements is probably even more important if you believe a crime has occurred, and your company intends to report the matter to the police. The police detectives and others reviewing your findings will be examining the proof with an eye towards a possible prosecution (with a criminal conviction as its goal). Structuring your investigation this way is like giving them a road map to proving the crime, identifying areas for them to supplement with their own fact-finding, and otherwise taking your case.

65) Interim measures are meant to help. Don't let them hurt.

When serious allegations of misconduct are directed toward a specific employee, your company may need to take preliminary action pending the completion of your investigation. If necessary to protect the health and safety of any employee, to protect the integrity of the company's policies and procedures, or even the need to simply "stop the action" until the investigation is done, management may consider taking any of the following steps:

- Suspension of the implicated person, with or without pay.
- Sending the employee home without a suspension, but on a paid leave of absence until the matter can be reviewed.
- Temporary transfer of an employee pending the completion of the investigation.

Interim measures, however, are not cost-free, even when needed. If the implicated person is alerted to the allegation, which is inevitable if he or she is suspended or terminated before you can interview them, the likelihood of a successful confrontation in an investigation is diminished, especially if the employee retains a lawyer. Proactive measures to obtain damaging evidence against the employee through surveillance or similar measures will, in all likelihood, be lost. The employee may also try to influence other witnesses or third parties who know of the misconduct, or the employee may try to destroy relevant documents or other evidence.

You must recognize that there will be circumstances where the company will have no choice but to suspend or terminate the employee at the same time you are trying to figure out what happened. However, in the absence of a genuine threat to the company's financial well-being, the better option for your investigation is to wait with the interim steps until the confrontational interview with the subject has taken place. Whatever the choice, interim steps must be coordinated between you, Human Resources, and executive management.

You can be creative with interim measures and tailor them to your specific needs. An employee has no right to continue working unaffected by the investigation. It is only wrong to penalize them if the investigation has not yet been completed. This might seem unfair to some people, but investigations are one of the realities of being a corporate employee.

An investigator must weigh the options to ensure that the investigation is not hampered by interim steps. Suspending or terminating an employee severely limits the investigator's ability to confront the employee under conditions carefully designed and structured to maximize the likelihood of a confession. As with other factors in the investigations process, decisions made regarding interim measures should be the result of a conscious, informed decision. And be prepared to defend the interim measures both to the implicated person and the department affected by the person's absence.

66) You're going to be a guest in someone's house.
Tell the managers.

Word of an investigation usually spreads rapidly through the department under investigation. Unless there is a specific need to conceal the existence of the investigation from senior management in the relevant department, courtesy and professionalism dictate that you notify them before the first interview starts. A solid, professional start is particularly important when you anticipate that you'll need their assistance facilitating interviews and locating documents during the investigation.

If the initial notice is oral, your investigative file should reflect who was contacted. A personal courtesy visit early in the investigation is also helpful to establish good rapport.

During the personal visit, you might advise the department's leaders of the general nature of the allegations, or you may state the specific allegations if you don't believe that will compromise the investigation. Department heads should not be told of the reporter's identity, or allowed to review or make copies of any correspondence from the reporter, unless the case file clearly shows the reporter earlier agreed to it. (Many investigators prefer not to provide this information to management even when the reporter does not object.)

During the courtesy visit, it is appropriate to remind managers not to discuss the investigation with others, especially witnesses, and to be careful to avoid any action that someone could construe, fairly or not, as retaliation for initiating or cooperating with the investigation.

67) Good interviews only come from good investigators.

The interview is usually the most important part of any investigation. People are generally the best source of information. Somebody usually knows all the important details of the major points of your investigation. Other witnesses usually have enough knowledge to fill in the smaller factual gaps.

But obtaining the maximum possible information depends on whether you can elicit the information needed. If you are poorly trained or lack specialized experience—in an investigation that requires it—the investigation will suffer. The same is true when interview tasks are delegated to colleagues who don't have the requisite skills.

Some people in your company may be natural conversationalists, or they may have regular interaction with customers and colleagues. But speaking to people is not the same as interviewing them. Effective questioning techniques are not learned in related disciplines (like law or human resources) or polite society. The skills are learned only from specialized training bolstered through experience.

So make sure you take the time and make the effort to become a good investigator. Your investigation depends on it.

68) Always ask: Why did he think he could get away with it? What's missing that would have allowed this? And how did he think he could escape detection?

It sounds ironic, but investigations can also be too factually detailed. We can focus too much on the substance of the implicated person's conduct. Did the accounts-payable clerk forge her boss's signature and cash the checks? Once we have established sufficient facts to prove the forgery, we close the investigation and move on.

But you may contribute more value if you explore a little more deeply. Let us assume the clerk is rational. She would not have forged the signature and cashed the checks if she believed she would be caught. So why didn't she believe that she would? How did she get so daring? The answers to those questions will give you a lot of insight into what is really going on, and what really needs to be fixed.

Statistics from the Association of Certified Fraud Examiners show both that workplace fraud continues until it is detected, and the amounts stolen grow over time. Understanding the dynamics clearly as soon as possible can really protect your company by allowing process improvements to be made as soon as possible.

69) As with real estate, it's location, location, location.

Choose a good interview location, because of its effect on the witness and, consequently, on the information he gives you. A witness who fears that his co-workers may hear what he says or see him speaking to you will not give you all the information you might otherwise gather if he believed he could speak freely. A witness who feels very comfortable and protected in his statements is likely to share more with you than even he intended. Once people start speaking comfortably, their natural protective defenses begin to drop. A good investigator senses these changes and probes deeper for more-valuable information.

The location of the interview should be a neutral place that is conducive to effective information-gathering and protects the fairness of the process. Forget the stereotype of the bare room, single chair and spotlight. It makes for good theater, but intimidating settings actually make people less likely to share information. You may think an intimidated witness feels compelled to give you more information. But that becomes a question of quantity, not quality. An intimidated witness is more likely to lie or evade probing questions because he fears you and the investigation process. Pressure tactics frequently backfire, undermine your integrity and credibility, and might even lead to an ethics claim against you.

Pressure tactics are also intellectually lazy. The reality is that the more comfortable people are, the more they open up to you. The interview locations should therefore be a relatively benign environment, and the witness should be physically free to get up and leave at any time. The room should be at normal temperature and should be free of distractions. The key is to make an informed choice for the best interview spot possible. Each venue has its advantages and disadvantages. These change depending on the allegation, the business need to display to others that a workplace investigation is being conducted, and the particular witness you are interviewing.

Interviews in restaurants or other public places pose distractions and risks to confidentiality. However, their advantage is that these venues can put a witness at ease because of its public, non-worksite nature. An off-site location might also be chosen if there is any concern about a disruption in the workplace as a result of confronting the witness. This is especially relevant when interrogating the implicated person.

Sometimes you will have multiple options for an interview location (like when you conduct them at the office) and sometimes you won't (like when the interview must be taken at an airport because it's the only time a witness is available). The key is to make an informed choice of venue while appreciating that each location has characteristics that will affect the dynamics of the interview.

70) You must control the interview, or the witness will.

Assert control in the beginning of an interview and keep it. Most interviews are one-on-one. The usual dynamic in these conversations is that one person leads, and one person follows. You have to be the leader. Otherwise, the witness determines how much information you will receive from the interview. This dynamic might happen not only with an implicated person who is trying to evade your probing questions. It could be any witness, such as a busy executive, who wants to tell you as little as possible and get out of there.

Keep control by being a critical listener. Asking follow-up questions based on precisely what the witness just told you gently remind the witness that you remain in control of the interview process. Conversely, just asking rote questions alerts the witness that you are just going through the motions, and he should just give you the answer that helps him the most and allows him to get out of there quickly.

On a related topic, never underestimate the mental or physical abilities of your witness. When you do that actively (by assuming the witness is unimportant or useless) or passively (you're too tired or busy to pay much attention), you do more than risk denying yourself valuable information. You also undermine the investigations process by communicating to the witness that the process—along with the stereotypes of avenging angels and finger pointers—is more important than he is.

Workplace investigations are intended to reduce unacceptable business risks which, it is hoped, result in a safer and more-productive work environment. If the witness will be a beneficiary of the work environment your investigation is trying to improve, doesn't the investigation serve him, not vice versa?

So operate under the belief that the person being interviewed is intelligent and important. Never show any degree of contempt unless you are using it deliberately as an interviewing tactic to gain more information.

71) Make an informed witness list.

You don't want to speak to every possible witness. Decide which witnesses will likely give you the information you need to substantiate each element of the allegation. This will help you narrow your witness list to include only the essential ones. The temptation to interview everyone who could be possibly relevant to the investigation scope usually has more to do with a poor investigation plan rather than a desire for thoroughness. So if you cannot articulate what relevant information you might get from the witness, don't schedule the interview. Don't pick someone for an interview based on little more than a "hey, you never know" standard.

Once you construct your witness list, you need to decide on the ideal interview order. (The order is "ideal" because it is more your aspiration than anything else. Interview order depends heavily on witness availability.) When you can, put your "skeleton witness" at the top of the list. This person is usually someone with good institutional knowledge of people and processes but who has no—or at most minimal—connections to the underlying facts. This person helps you establish the basic framework of the information you hope to develop from the interviews—hence the clever name—and the other witnesses just fill in the flesh on the skeleton.

72) You don't know 98 percent about your witnesses.

You usually interview your colleagues, so it is easy to assume that you understand them and what makes them tick. After all, you work for the same company, right? Wrong.

Most witnesses are strangers and, even if you know them, you really don't know that much about them. You don't really know what goes on in their private lives, what problems exist at home, what personal goals are not being satisfied at the office. So don't assume anything or project your own values, life experience or personal motivations on someone else. It is true that each of us acts rationally, but what is rational for you may not be rational for someone else. Let the facts, not your projected assumptions, explain what motivated someone.

Similarly, be cautious about what others tell you about the witness. The information colleagues know might be fabrications choreographed by the witness. It may also be gossip, speculation or office legend.

Finally, because you truly know so little about them, you should avoid the temptation to speak ill of colleagues when you proved the misconduct. You don't walk in their shoes.

73) No one makes a report out of good corporate citizenship.

People report actual or possible misconduct for a variety of reasons. A reporter may be a resigning employee who wants either to take a parting shot at someone or share information that he now feels liberated to disclose. A reporter may be someone who feels aggrieved by a lost promotion or bonus. A reporter may be someone who believes that throwing someone else under the bus is a good way to advance their career. A reporter may also be someone who, having participated in wrongdoing, reports others in order to distance themselves from it. The one thing you should remember is that a report is rarely made only to protect the company's interests.

General uncertainty about the reporter's true motives—you probably never knew the reporter before that moment—means you should keep an objective distance and assume nothing beyond your intention to conduct a thorough inquiry. The inquiry must include understanding the reporter's motives. You must always consider the reporter's motives because motives affect credibility. An ignoble motive, however, doesn't necessarily mean the report is fabricated. It only means that you need to scrutinize why the reporter has contacted you, as well as what he is telling you.

In some cases, the reporter should be considered more like an informer for law enforcement (there's that criminal-justice comparison again): someone who gives information because of a definite personal gain or motive. The motivations may be varied. Generally, motivations fall into these categories: revenge, reward, repentance, and ego. Whatever the motives, be sure to learn which ones motivated your reporter.

74) Give standard witness instructions.

Most of the employees you interview will be nervous and understandably apprehensive. Each has probably never been interviewed before. This gives you an opportunity to control the interview at the outset and put it on a productive path. The introduction to the interview is the hardest part because you have to create the proper impression, and enlist the witness's cooperation to learn the relevant facts the witness is expected to provide.

Witnesses are generally nervous strangers who don't know what to expect. If they have made any assumptions about the interview, they probably aren't positive ones. All the more reason to give a standard set of instructions at the beginning to establish ground rules for the interview.

Giving clear interview instructions conveys to witnesses that you are in control of the interview and they are not. Standard instructions show a consistent business practice. If a witness later denies you gave them instructions or disputes what instructions you gave, you can defend your position by pointing to this regular business practice. (Once again, this protects an investigator's downside risks by anticipating and possibly preempting a problem.)

The witness should receive a brief explanation of the matter under investigation. Explain why the witness has been included in the investigation (that he has been identified as someone with a report, has been a subject of misconduct, or has been identified as someone who may have information relevant to the investigation).

Standard instructions help both the investigation and the investigator. They should be the first step of any interview.

75) Never take the reporter's information at face value.

In most investigations, the reporter is a stranger as are the people about whom he is reporting. You probably know little more than the facts of the report. Besides the reporter's motives for making the report, you do not know if his characterizations are even remotely accurate. Reporters usually offer conclusions about the behavior they report, such as "my boss discriminates against me." Few reporters offer the facts without their own interpretation of what the facts showed.

So what do you do? Just focus on the facts of the report, and skip over the editorializing and commentary. Look for complete answers and full descriptions. Identify participants and possible witnesses. You can quite easily accept the facts without the spin.

A reporter interview, unlike other interviews, seeks to establish probable cause for the investigation. This means you also need to know facts that undercut the possibility misconduct didn't occur. Probe for weaknesses by asking reporters what they expect the implicated person to say in defense of his actions, and why such a response is not sufficient to dispose of the matter. Questions like these might show that probable cause does not exist or, to the contrary, it might help identify why the complained-about conduct might have no legitimate business justification.

Your job is neither to vouch for the reporter nor accept his information at face value and run with it. The reporter is only an important information source who should be probed thoroughly.

76) Ask why the reporter didn't call the hotline.

Regardless of how your company positions your hotline—"tell us your workplace concerns" or "call us only if you are sure the CFO is a crook"—it remains a significant source of reports for possible investigation. Your professional effectiveness depends on a robust use of that phone number.

When interviewing a reporter who contacted you through the hotline, the reporter's reasons for using it will be fairly obvious. Maybe he saw the posters, or remembered the number from the code of conduct, or someone in Human Resources gave it to him. But when the reporter comes to you from a different source, do you ask why he didn't call the hotline? Don't you want to know why?

Reporters who didn't use the hotline may offer a variety of reasons, all helpful to understanding some practical dynamics in your company. Do these people know the phone number and your company leadership's expectations for its use? If your company has a mandatory reporting policy, do the employees know about it? Do people doubt either that their anonymity will be protected or that the company will meaningfully respond to the report?

Knowing how your employees view the hotline in this real-world setting—instead of the numbers of posters and slices of "Compliance Day" cake distributed—will help you take the needed steps to ensure the hotline remains valuable and relevant to the business.

77) Anonymous reporters are neither unethical nor character assassins.

Choosing to remain anonymous does not mean that the initial report is made in bad faith. (The converse is equally true. Identified reporters are not always paragons of virtue.) It seems ridiculous, therefore, that executives in some companies piously state that a reporter must have the courage to identify himself before the company should consider the report seriously.

Reporters often choose to remain anonymous because (1) they fear retaliation for making the report, and (2) they are skeptical that anything will change if they report their concerns. In a sense, these reporters are blaming those pious executives for not practicing what they preach to others in the company.

Companies should always encourage people to identify themselves and report their concerns. However, it is not unethical to make a report anonymously and, under some conditions, it might even be reasonable. Anonymity is not a significant problem for you if a reporter wants to stay that way. (Incidentally, many anonymous reporters self-identify when an investigator's professionalism and commitment to confidentiality become apparent, and the reporter no longer fears retaliation.) What you care about is the information and the basis for that person's knowledge. If you get information from a credible witness, the person's name is not that important.

78) Don't identify anonymous reporters.

An identified reporter is easier. But never actively try to identify anonymous reporters. Anonymous reporters frequently identify themselves later. If you compose a good witness list, the anonymous reporter will likely be one of your witnesses during the fact-finding phase. Don't undermine the promised anonymity of your hotline by doing anything to make people believe that they will be identified.

So if the reporter is anonymous and cannot be interviewed, do what you can in other ways to learn about the report. If the report specifies a branch office, speak to its manager. If a co-worker is named in the report, check with his or her supervisor or Human Resources. The reporter is only one source of information even when identified. There may still be other sources of information for you to check if you need them.

79) Manage the reporter's expectations.

Disappoint reporters early and often. In other words, manage their expectations carefully. Ask the reporter what he wants you to do about the report. Asking the question gives you an opportunity to tell the reporter whether his expectation of what you can or will do in the case is realistic.

If the reporter tells you he only wants to share his concerns but does not want an investigation conducted, inform the reporter that, depending on the information, your company may have a legal obligation to investigate. His preferences are immaterial.

Keep in mind that a reporter will rarely contact you the minute misconduct has occurred. The more likely scenario is a litany of events that have allowed the reporter's feelings to fester. By the time you learn about it, the reporter feels sufficiently aggrieved. The passage of time probably reinforced the reporter's desire for some specific redress. He may want the bonus or promotion he feels he has been denied, he may want to see someone fired, or he may want a nice cash payment by your company to compensate for the injustice he claims to have suffered.

But you are a company representative, not an ombudsman. Your obligation is to identify misconduct in the company so that it can be addressed. You do not conduct your investigations to redress the grievances of a company employee. The investigation protects the company by identifying areas of unacceptable business risk. The investigation is not a dispute-resolution service.

You properly manage expectations when you explain your proper role in the process, and what the reporter should expect as a result of your efforts. Whatever you choose to say, don't end your critical discussions by leaving the reporter speculating about what you might be able to do for him. You may expose yourself and the company to further problems if the reporter eventually believes, because you were not clear enough, that you didn't do what he thought you would because you chose instead to whitewash the misconduct you investigated.

The reporter is entitled to have you accept the report and consider whether a workplace investigation is warranted. Any other reporter benefit is simply a by-product of your efforts.

80) You can't un-ring a bell. Recanting reporters don't stop investigations.

Sometimes a reporter is angry, upset, or otherwise passionate about making a report to the Compliance Department. During the intake process, the reporter finds his concerns validated by a compliance professional—validating, however, does not necessarily mean agreeing with them—and this brings the reporter's stress level down. The reporter now starts becoming concerned that, despite your company's non-retaliation policy, his identity will be learned, and he will be a future victim of retaliation. The reporter's information has clearly established probable cause to justify an investigation, but now he has buyer's remorse. The reporter wants to withdraw the report and have you forget the whole thing.

The simple answer is that you can't forget it. You are a management representative. Someone with personal knowledge—the reporter—has made a credible report to you of possible misconduct. The company, therefore, is on notice of possible employee wrongdoing. Your investigation is based on that information, not the reporter's willingness to cooperate. Therefore, the investigation must continue. You cannot un-ring the bell.

81) When in doubt, start with what you know and work outward.

It's easy to plan an investigation when its objective seems obvious and the corresponding business needs for your fact-finding are clear. But not every case is that straightforward. You may be assigned an investigation that seems to have no particular starting point, such as a reporter who resists your efforts to be interviewed for initial information. It may also seem that, in the initial stages, you know very little about the dimensions of the problems and whether an investigation is warranted. It may feel that there is much to be learned but you don't know how to get there.

Let's consider a practical example. You receive a hotline report from an anonymous reporter. Although you left a message on your company's hotline system asking the reporter to contact you for more information, the reporter has not responded. The report alleges that a particular company manager unprofessionally favors the female colleagues and ignores their male co-workers. The report identifies both the manager and the location of the company office. However, the report contains a veiled threat to go to the media if you don't address the problem right away. You can't determine if the report concerns sexual harassment or just poor management supervision. What do you do?

When the path seems unclear, focus on what you do know, and work your way in. In this example, you know the manager and the office. Check with someone you trust who is uninvolved with the facts—in other words, someone who is neither implicated nor has fact-specific information, and ask for a high-level assessment of the department and the situation. Check with Human Resources. Maybe someone there received similar reports in the past, or perhaps the department has had past problems with this manager. (Please notice the distinction between asking about the existence of earlier reports or stated concerns and a what-do-you-think fishing expedition.)

If all you initially know are the little details, then start there. To misuse a metaphor, don't just dive into the deep end of the pool—such as rushing to the office and interviewing anyone you can find—and hope you can find something to latch on to. Start at the edges and work your way in.

82) The more specific you are in a case, the more general everything becomes.

This topic may sound like a contradiction, but it is not. Investigations are not mechanical. The facts that lead to a determination that misconduct has occurred come from an analysis of personal conduct. The closer you examine that conduct, with the deeper insights that come from a close examination, the better you understand the personal dynamics that facilitated the misconduct.

For example, you are investigating an office manager who is accused of violating the code of conduct's "Mutual Respect" provision. The general consensus of her co-workers is that she is a petty tyrant who micromanages everyone and everything. But as you dive deeper, you find that her supervisor regularly encouraged her behavior as a way to manipulate and control others in the office. The boss lets her do his dirty work, and he in turn looks like a saint by comparison. You also find out that she hates being placed in that position, but that the supervisor forces her to play along.

By looking so specifically at the situation, you made a more-general observation that the entire department is operationally dysfunctional and that other employees may be similarly manipulated. You are now able to make concrete recommendations to remedy the operational issues. This would not have happened if you had not first sought the granularity that comes with doing a "deep dive."

83) Don't interview everyone.

Interviews are often the best sources of information in any investigation. But you can't keep interviewing indefinitely. Any reluctance to stop interviewing likely comes from a poor investigation plan that failed to articulate precisely what you sought to learn. But let's be more positive and assume you made a good plan. Therefore, consider yourself finished when, based on your experience and training, you reasonably believe that we have gathered sufficient information to meet the burden of proof, and that there is not some important document or person unexamined which may have material information.

Cumulative witnesses—those people who simply repeat known information without adding anything more—also pose a process risk. The human memory is not perfect, and truthful witnesses may have different recollections of the same event. What will you do if they contradict each other? How will you proceed then?

This is not to suggest you take a narrow approach and stop asking questions the moment you hear what you are looking for. The point is that layering witnesses only for the sake of thoroughness but not for gathering additional information can backfire. Each witness should address a specific need in your fact finding. If you cannot articulate that need before the interview starts, maybe you shouldn't proceed with the interview.

84) Never give a witness a questionnaire or anything else before the interview.

Questionnaires tip off the witness to the areas you consider important. When provided in advance, questionnaires give the witness plenty of time to concoct an answer.

A questionnaire can be effectively used, however, when you only need specific questions answered from a non-critical witness. This may save you time and effort because it avoids the need for a personal interview. It also helps because it creates a written document response that you can simply drop in the file.

Just remember that questionnaires serve only a limited purpose for your investigation.

85) Be smart in an interview, but don't outsmart yourself.

A good investigator utilizes many of his personal traits, but he must be able to adjust his own style to harmonize with the traits and moods of the witness. Once again, flexibility serves you well.

There are many errors that an investigator can make while adding his touches. Some of the more common are:

- Showing personal prejudice or allowing prejudice to influence the conduct of the interview. This destroys your objectivity and credibility.
- Lying destroys your credibility and encourages similar behavior from the witness.
- Hurrying encourages mistakes and omissions and leads you to evaluate improperly the veracity of the information provided.
- Making assumptions, drawing unconfirmed inferences, or jumping to conclusions may result in important information not being requested or allow false or unverifiable information to be introduced into the investigation.
- Making promises you can't keep. This destroys your credibility and may cause the witness to react negatively to other investigative personnel in the future.
- Looking down at or degrading the witness. Showing a contemptuous attitude may anger the witness and encourage unnecessary emotional barriers.
- Placing too much value on minor inconsistencies allows you to get "hung up" on minor or irrelevant issues.
- Bluffing destroys your credibility and may allow the witness to take charge of the interview when the bluff is exposed.
- Anger results in your surrendering control to the witness. It helps the witness and is a distraction from the information-gathering process.
- Underestimating the mental abilities of the witness antagonizes him and invites him to try to trip you up.

A smart investigator has no use for these tactics. A professional knows they serve no productive purpose.

86) You lie, you're fired.

Lying witnesses pose two risks to an investigator. First, the falsehoods deny you relevant information and send you off pursuing leads in the wrong places. Second, proven falsehoods destroy the credibility of the witness on those topics on which he might have been telling you the truth.

People will lie to you if they believe that lying will help them more than telling you the truth. It stands to reason, therefore, that a good way to get the truth in an interview is to convince the witness that telling the truth will be better for him than lying.

The good news is that lying is not a natural human behavior. Lying must be done consciously. But don't jump to conclusions about the reasons the witness may be lying. Liars have plenty of reasons to do it. But you must try to understand what motivates the lies so you can overcome them. Is it a fear of getting involved? Is the witness lying because he fears retaliation from the implicated person or being labeled a "rat?" Does the witness have some minor culpability that he now fears you will link to the larger problem under investigation? If you can understand the motive, you might be able to overcome it and get truthful testimony.

Your company needs a zero-tolerance rule for lying to an investigator during a company investigation. Otherwise, there is no real penalty for lying in the interview or evading responsibility.

The zero-tolerance rule is good as a basic rule for employees in investigations—as with similar rules, who in your company leadership would oppose it?—but it has limited practical value. If you are investigating issues so you can explain them and offer business-focused assistance, firing someone for lying, however justified, doesn't get you information. You need to see a lying witness instead as a challenge, not an opportunity for a "gotcha" moment to get him fired.

If you cannot overcome the witness's desire to lie to you, the integrity of the investigations process requires you to address his falsehood. But you will still have to prove the lie. You will need sufficient facts to show that the witness made a deliberate misstatement of fact that was intended to deceive or mislead you. This can be done by assembling sufficient contradictory testimony or circumstantial proof to show, by a preponderance of evidence, that the witness's statement was knowingly false.

A lying witness does not help you gather the relevant facts to give business-focused advice, so you must try to sidestep the lie or persuade the witness that the truth helps him more. It's better to encourage the witness to rationalize his behavior in some factual context—like the proverbial hangover which seemed like a good idea the night before—than fight the lie. Admissions of fact would show misconduct, however rationalized. These admissions will bring you closer to your objective.

87) The witness can't speak if you do.

Investigators tend to speak more than we should in an interview. We try to reassure nervous witnesses. We explain our bona fides and how the inquiries are legitimate. We apologize for being there and disrupting the department's business operations. We apologize for taking them away from their duties. We explain how the witness fits into the inquiries. We profusely justify certain lines of questioning. This may make us feel better about the intrusion, but none of this generates evidence for our investigation.

Remember the 80:20 rules. You are there to acquire knowledge, not disclose it. The witness should be talking 80 percent of the time, and you only approximately 20 percent of the time. Allow the witness to tell his own story. Don't rush to anticipate and preempt collateral questions about the investigation process. Invite the witness to ask any questions he may have, and then just respond accordingly.

If you hear your own voice too much, that's a signal. Let the witness speak. You came to hear him, not vice versa.

88) Keep it simple.

Each interview should convey relevant information clearly and efficiently. Questions should be straightforward and grammatically simple. Answers should be limited to facts based on personal—or possibly second-hand—knowledge. Never use language the witness cannot understand.

Interview answers lose their clarity, and therefore utility, when you use words that are vague, ambiguous or overly technical. You must also avoid questions that are capable of multiple interpretations and not accept answers that are similarly vulnerable.

This goal is about more than just avoiding ambiguity. Workplace interviews face two common risks. First, most companies develop their own acronyms and colloquialisms—either homegrown or part of the latest corporate fads. Does "QPR" mean quarterly performance review or quantity per revenue? What is a "paradigm?" Even if you, as one of their colleagues, know what the witness likely means, confirm it for the record anyway. Make sure you're both talking about the same thing. There is always the possibility that the interview may be used beyond the limited scope of your investigation.

The second risk is when investigators and witnesses use legalistic words—like "unethical," "assault," "battery," etc.—that are loaded with meaning and component elements. When inserted in a question, the witness might not understand what you mean, even if you do. When inserted in an answer, you may interpret the answer differently than the witness intended because you knew what the word means, and perhaps the witness didn't.

Direct answers, stated clearly and without ambiguity, make the best proof.

89) Different interview questions yield different answers.

A smart witness is not going to help you. At best, a witness is going to respond truthfully and to the best of his ability. But the answer, however truthful and complete, still depends on the precise question you ask. Knowing how to use different questions is like knowing how to use a special code to unlock information. There are two main types of questions:

- Closed questions usually require a simple yes or no answer, or an undeniable fact such as name, address, phone number, etc. When used at the beginning of an interview, these questions encourage affirmative responses. When used later on, closed questions lock the witness into important details.
- Open questions begin with a stated (or implied) who, where, what, when, how and why. An open question cannot be answered with a yes or no. It requires some narrative explanation by the witness. Open questions reveal the greatest amount of information because they convey the most detail.

There are other types of questions, of course. But the open and closed questions illustrate a crucial point for investigators: you control the answers more than you may think. The completeness of an answer, whether yes, no or a narrative explanation, depends on your question, not the willingness of the witness to disclose information. So frame your questions carefully.

90) There are no magic questions.

There are no "magic questions" to ask when interviewing someone. But framing good interview questions becomes easier when you conceptualize the interview rather than just list relevant topics to cover. For example, if you view the aggregate information of the investigation as painting a landscape, which part of the landscape does the witness fill? Or see it as a jigsaw puzzle. Which piece is this witness? The goal of any interview is to place the witness within the operative fact scenarios you are investigating. Once you see it this way, each interview will be more effective than just gathering individual answers to discrete questions.

As a practical matter, you will never fail if you ask "who, what, where, when, why and how" questions. But don't ask "why" questions until the end. These questions generally seem antagonistic because they sound moralistic. These questions may appear as finger-pointing to discourage the now-defensive witness from giving full information.

The best question you can ask, however, is "so then what happened?" This question encourages a narrative answer, which will point you towards follow-up and more specific answers to key details. It also allows you to proceed chronologically, which helps you keep the facts straight and follows the way people normally remember events.

91) Don't use an interview script.

Although you no doubt want to ask all the right questions, an interview script keeps you more focused on the questions you ask rather than the answers you receive. Effective interviewing requires you to be an active listener, on alert for dissembling, awkward answers to straightforward questions, as well as the common signs of deception.

If you are confident in your ability to be an active listener, consider making a list of topics to cover with that witness. This list should be a subset of the complete list of topics you need to cover with the aggregate of your witnesses. The list should be constantly updated as you progress through your witness list.

A good investigator seeks the flexibility to think, listen and watch as the interview unfolds. Scripts unfortunately encourage a mechanical, check-the-box approach to fact-finding. (Once again, you need to adjust and adapt as the information comes in.) Scripts also cause you to over-control the investigation. You instead want to stay loose enough so you can observe, calibrate and refine your questioning.

There are three exceptions to this approach. First, when interrogating your implicated person, you'll probably seek specific factual admissions—such as, "when you allowed your brother-in-law to be a company vendor, you never told your boss about your family connection, did you?" In these situations, composing the precise question in advance is necessary because the admission is an important part of your proof. If your findings, it is hoped, include admissions by the implicated person, you cannot base the findings on a generalized confession of culpability. You need to pin the implicated person down on specifics.

This point is important. Specific admissions are relevant to understanding motive (important to you) and mitigating circumstances (important to him). There is a significant difference—at least in terms of giving business-focused advice—between someone who falsified his expense report because a recent divorce left him impoverished and someone who did it because people in the department know their boss rubber-stamps everything and condones padded expense accounts as a hidden part of employee compensation.

Second, if you plan to refer your findings to the police after the investigation is completed, the police will consider specific admissions far more probative of criminal activity than just your determination that a misconduct allegation is substantiated. (This assessment has much to do with the higher beyond-a-reasonable-doubt standard.)

Third, use an interview script where the witness—whether implicated or not—is expected to give you anything other than rambling answers that seem to do everything other than answer a straightforward question. The witness may be nervous, evasive or simply prone to communicate this way. Asking closed questions—with specific facts for which you seek short or yes-or-no answers—may be the only way productively to develop the information the witness offers you.

92) Stay flexible. There is no checklist for everything.

Investigating is easier when you've given some thought to what you think may have happened. The key phrase is "may have." Although your initial hunch will likely be different from what you eventually learn, having something to aim at is better than having no target at all.

Your initial theory about what likely happened is called your "floating hypothesis." The floating hypothesis changes as additional information is learned and continues to be refined until all the facts are developed. A floating hypothesis, however, is not the same as rushing to judgment about the misconduct. It is intended to give some focus to your inquiries while you keep an open mind about what you will eventually learn. Like a scientific hypothesis, you develop the facts to confirm or, if necessary, disprove it.

93) Blend multiple witnesses to obscure who told you.

You are investigating the manager of a small department in your company. Because of its size, everyone seems to know everyone. When you interview Mary, she gives you detailed valuable information because she wants the problem to be resolved. The source of that information will obviously appear to be Mary once the others hear about it. Your problem is that you want to avoid any actual or perceived retaliation against Mary from people who might consider her a "rat." If even the perception of retaliation arises, future witnesses may clam up, and people you've already interviewed may recant their testimony to avoid any problems. So what do you do?

This situation presents a practical problem. The usual admonitions against retaliation should be given, of course, but the effective operation of the department requires you to do something more than just give warnings. In these situations, consider blending multiple witness statements. Take the important facts of Mary's statement, and mix it with the less-important information of other witnesses. Ask questions based on Mary's information—the ones you really care about—and questions based on the others. Essentially cover your interviewing tracks.

During the interview, you may come to believe the witness suspects it is Mary or generally want to know the source of the information. To counteract this, consider two steps. First, advise the witness preemptively—another expression of your control of the interview—that your questions are an amalgam of information from multiple witnesses, so he shouldn't think that all the information came from one person he may, or may not, be able to identify. Second, if the witness directly asks you who gave you that information, simply decline to do so. Emphasize that the accuracy of the information, not its source, is the important factor.

94) Even if you ask the right questions, you still have to listen for the right answer.

An effective investigator is an active listener. An active listener tries to grasp the meaning of what is being said, and also what isn't being said. He signals acceptance to the witness, which, in turn, sends a message to the witness that it is okay to speak. He shows genuine interest, but he does not inject his opinions, value judgments and criticisms.

A witness's response has two possibilities. You have to be alert to concrete information in order to develop an objective explanation for the matter under investigation. You also have to be alert to abstract information in order to sift out emotional, nonspecific, and sometimes misleading information. Abstract information can also be the basis for additional questioning that leads to concrete information.

So how does an investigator communicate active listening to the witness in order to encourage complete answers? By taking each of these steps:

- Maintain a body language—posture, movement, gestures, and facial expressions—that signals active participation in the interview.
- Maintain eye contact to help the flow of information. Eye contact signals that it is time to answer.
- Maintain a positive silence. Silence can be perceived as a sign of rejection and displeasure. But used right, it can show you accept the witness and that you control the interview.

Interviewing requires more than just asking good questions. There are multiple dimensions to human communication. You want to use all of them to your advantage.

95) Cover your tracks.

Most parts of an investigation benefit from transparency: the purpose of the investigation, the business needs and likely post-investigation steps, to name a few. There are some parts of the investigation, however, where transparency might not serve your investment goals.

During the interview, and similar to when you don't want to attribute facts to any one witness, it usually helps if you do not call attention to any specific topic as being more important than others. If the witness knows the areas you believe are critical, you face two risks. First, if the topic about which you have signaled concern is one that might implicate the witness in misconduct, the witness now knows that he should evade or make misstatements about these topics to avoid implicating himself. Although the witness may have been evasive anyway, you've guaranteed it now. (The witness might have been modestly truthful if he figured his testimony would just be buried among the volume of information you are gathering.)

The second risk arises if the witness committed misconduct but not the specific misconduct about which you are primarily concerned. If you signal the topic you care about and his misconduct is somewhere else, he knows he's in the clear. But if he doesn't know, there is always a chance he might admit his own misconduct either to put his own spin on the facts or to offer mitigating details.

Remember that these concerns must be balanced with other interview dynamics. Covering your tracks, so to speak, does not preclude you from giving sufficient details to the witness to focus his recollections and testimony. It is just another example of the dynamics to be considered when conducting an effective interview.

So order your interview topics in a way that does not call attention to particular problem areas. The order of questions as well as your demeanor in asking them should never alert a witness to precisely what you think is critical as well as the severity of the problem under investigation. If there is something you would prefer to remain highly confidential, take care in structuring and asking the questions to the witness. (Some experienced investigators even include subjects of no real relevance to cover their tracks.)

96) Silence makes people speak.

Silence is a great technique. Many people cannot stand silence and find this unnerving. (Count to ten silently and see how it feels.) A witness may fill up the void with talk, possibly saying something he had no intention of revealing. The average person expects no more than seven seconds of silence during a conversation. So if you don't say anything after the witness answers a question, a witness will frequently offer you more information on that question. The silence effectively communicates that you think the answer was incomplete. Silence can also be an effective way to undermine a witness who is cocky and confident in his ability to control the discussion.

Remember, however, that you may become vulnerable to the same thing. If a witness significantly pauses, you might be tempted to fill the silence. Consequently, you could cut off the possibility of additional witness information or start explaining things to the witness that you didn't intend to disclose. The witness, and not you, should become uncomfortable with the silence. Use the moment to get a drink of water or briefly to rest your voice.

97) There can be no quid pro quo for cooperating in an interview.

You conduct interviews because you seek facts. Witnesses, of course, have the information but sometimes fear to share it because it might get them in trouble. As a business-focused investigator, you are more interested in fixing business problems than in nailing employees for not-too-serious misconduct. So if a witness offers to tell you everything you want to know if (1) he won't be fired, (2) he won't be sued to recover the ill-gotten gains, and/ or (3) you won't call the cops, isn't that a good deal? No.

Never, ever make a *quid pro quo* promise. Although it might sound like a good way to wrap up the investigation, it may be illegal. The offer not to do something harmful to someone (e.g., go to the police) in exchange for something of value (e.g., their information) is technically extortion.

When the potential for a *quid pro quo* offer arises, you must make it abundantly clear to the witness that his information, however welcome, does not affect a decision by your company to contact the police, start a lawsuit or take similar action. You must explain that these are separate considerations, and one may not be linked to the other.

Of course, this begs the next question of, why should the witness say anything? If this question gets asked, explain that you are trying to understand what happened and why. Frequently, things look more sinister than they turn out to be. (Corporate life is usually pretty mundane.) The witness may choose to decline to speak further, but you can explain that then you will not have the benefit of his information. That information might include mitigating circumstances that put the relevant events in a more-accurate context.

It may seem like a bad choice to turn down a witness's offer, especially when the likelihood of a successful civil suit to recover the money or a successful prosecution is remote. Unfortunately, you have no alternative.

98) Employees have to cooperate with your investigations.

It is not surprising that people don't want to get involved with your investigations. Only the motivated ones want to speak to you. An implicated person wants to avoid being interviewed so his wrongdoing won't be discovered. He may even claim some Fifth Amendment right to remain silent (which does not apply to private-sector employment.) A witness who has relevant information but is not implicated may not want to speak to you for fear either of exposing himself to discipline or appearing like a tattletale. The witness, however, has little choice.

Your employer pays you to provide personal labor on its behalf. In return, you receive compensation. There are certain conditions on your employment. One of them is to act in the best interests of your employer.

Every employer is legally obligated to provide a safe and proper place to work. Besides obvious things like fire escapes and desk chairs that won't collapse, part of that obligation includes investigating misconduct when credible allegations arise. This is one of the ways to ensure a workplace free of unacceptable risks. Otherwise, your employer exposes itself to legal liability.

That's where you come in. If you are conducting an investigation, every employee has an obligation to cooperate because that employee would be assisting their employer to provide that safe and proper place to work. (We will assume it is a legitimate investigation based on probable cause.) So if an employee has relevant information or can otherwise assist your inquiries, he should do so upon your reasonable request.

Accordingly, cooperating with an investigation is a condition of employment. An employee can refuse to cooperate, and you cannot force him to. However, the employee may be terminated for refusing.

When you encounter a reluctant witness, don't go into bad-cop mode and start making threats. A reluctant witness may be trying to protect himself or someone else. Psychologists explain that people are often as reluctant to speak as negatively about themselves as they are about others. If you can create a sense of safety and acceptance—"I am just trying to understand what happened"—perhaps you might have better luck than threatening his continue employment.

A terminated employee is not going to be a witness, so your investigation gains no additional information if this rule gets enforced. So don't rely on it. Instead, explore why the witness refuses. You may be able to provide acceptable assurances or make accommodations that will overcome the witness's reluctance.

99) Believe in the self-fulfilling prophecy.

There are multiple dynamics at work during an interview. Among those dynamics are the ones that try to get witnesses to communicate effectively and furnish the information the investigator seeks. An effective dynamic is the self-fulfilling prophecy, also known as the "Pygmalion Effect."

The concept means that the projection of our expectation frequently produces that reality in others. For example, as we speak to witnesses, our attitude often determines how they respond. We are conveying our expectations to witnesses through our own conduct. This, in turn, influences how they behave in the interview.

An investigation can apply the technique a number of ways. The first way is your personal mental belief and expectation. In your questioning and attitude, you demonstrate to the witness your anticipation that he will cooperate.

The second way, not surprisingly, is to treat everyone as a valued human being. People often live up to the expectations of them.

The third way is to present your expectations subtly. Treat the witness as though he wants to comply. In other words, your attitude shows that you are not even considering that the witness may be reluctant to assist your inquiries.

The self-fulfilling prophecy also has an effect on you, and this is known as the "Galatea Effect." Employing this technique boosts your performance and enhances your own assessment of your skills.

100) Get the witness to admit policy up front.

Companies have lots of policies. The misconduct you frequently investigate will not be, as lawyers say, *malum in se,* or wrong itself. (For example, stealing is wrongful conduct, even in the absence of a company policy saying not to take company property.) Many company policies establish conduct as *malum prohibitum,* or wrong because it is declared to be wrong. (For example, a company policy that prohibits the accounts payable department from issuing checks over $5,000 without two signatures makes it wrongful conduct only because the company says it is.)

When investigating an allegation that an employee violated a *malum prohibitum* policy, it is a good first step to establish that the witness knows of the specific company policy. This is effective in two ways. First, if the witness denies knowing the policy that is integral to his job duties, he is admitting his own negligence in fulfilling his duties as an employee. Second, if the witness admits knowing the policy and you then prove he violated it, the allegation will be more easily substantiated and his misconduct becomes intentional.

101) Did you ever consider. . . . ?

Sometimes investigators are too focused on analyzing the rules. We identify the relevant company policy, and then we try to match it to the facts we are uncovering. This results in a very black-and-white review of what we believed happened. But the approach makes things two-dimensional because your investigation then explains only the policy and the conduct.

A similar situation arises when there is no precise policy for which you to base your inquiries. Sometimes, you will investigate management decision-making which, for some reason, violates either your code of conduct or the standards of professional management decision-making but no specific company policy.

Most workplace conduct under investigation involves employee decision-making. People make decisions for all kinds of reasons but, at least to them at that particular moment, those decisions are rational. In other words, at the time the decision was made, the person thought there was some reason that particular choice would benefit him.

When the department manager acknowledges that he made off-color jokes at the monthly meeting because he was trying to inject some levity into what would otherwise be a boring recitation of the recent sales data, explore his thought process. One of the most damning questions you can ever ask in an interview begins with "Did you ever consider..." In this example, the manager is faced with a Hobson's choice when the question is asked. He can admit that he considered the joke about the NFL cheerleaders to be appropriate in a business setting with male and female subordinates, thereby exposing his poor judgment. Or he can admit that he never considered its appropriateness at all, again exposing his poor judgment. Either way, you have added a third dimension to your inquiries by trying to explain what he was thinking.

This line of questioning is not a suggestion for you to play "gotcha" and try to embarrass your witness. The approach is helpful because it adds some context to the relevant decision-making. There are many reasons for the decisions we make in life, and those reasons are subjective. You should not presume to understand what motivated someone to act a certain way, and you should not simply presume onto the witness what would have motivated him in a similar situation.

Take your analysis one step further and add even more value.

102) Take all the time you need.

We are busy people. The witnesses have jobs to do, and only your job duties are being performed in the witness room. The witnesses want to get out of there (for multiple reasons), their bosses want you to wrap things up, and you probably have a plane to catch. Whatever the reasons, don't let the interview suffer as a result.

Do not stress time limits on the interview. Never give a time limit, because this rewards an evasive witness and discourages a witness who has lots of detail to give you. Make the witness believe that the company is sufficiently concerned about the matter. Conversely, do not accept unreasonable limits that would interfere with your ability to conduct a professional interview, such as the "busy" manager who can only give you a short amount of time. You are conducting a company investigation and, if needed, exercise your authority with the witness's supervisor to clear his calendar.

Finally, don't impose time limits on yourself. Plan your travel schedule accordingly. You cannot interview effectively if you keep staring at your watch and wondering if you can make it to the airport in time.

103) Know the advantages and disadvantages of a telephone interview.

Telephone interviews are common in a world of limited corporate resources. They can be used for minor investigations or minor witnesses without sacrificing too much investigative quality. But they will never replace an in-person interview. Telephone interviews have limited value and pose their own special risks.

Let's consider first the disadvantages of telephone interviews. You have a certain lack of control over the witness to direct the interview because he is not physically here with you. Although 70 percent of communication is through body language, you can only communicate verbally. You cannot see body language over the phone. If the witness is relying on notes or documents or someone giving them hand signals, you won't see that either. If someone is taping the interview despite your instructions not to, you won't see that. If the witness is silent for a period of time, you will not be able to determine what that means. And it can be harder to turn admissions into confessions by the implicated person who is interviewed over the phone.

Now, let's consider the advantages of telephone interviews. The witness can't read *your* body language. You can use a detailed outline and the witness will never know it. Your voice creates a sense of intimacy—Barry White would have been a terrific investigator—because the phone receiver will be held close to the witness's ear. This creates a sense of rapport and physical closeness. The interview can be taken by the most-appropriate investigator without concern about physical location. Other people can monitor the interview for training purposes. Telephone interviews also save time and money.

The key to a successful telephone interview is the ability to listen critically. You only have the witness's voice and words with which to work. Prepare to listen carefully, and focus on what is being said. Listen for facts, assumptions, personal judgments, possible bias, and especially key words and phrases. This allows you to maximize the value of a telephone interview.

104) Have the gall to ask uncomfortable questions.

Some investigations require you to ask uncomfortable questions to witnesses. This is unavoidable. In many investigations, the issues are provocative. Someone may be fired. Someone may not want to implicate a colleague. Someone may have done something terrible. But you still have to learn about it.

It is a normal human reaction to want to avoid asking tough or embarrassing questions. It takes a certain amount of gall to ask someone if he stole money, if he sent erotic messages to a co-worker, or if he forged company records. But conducting a proper investigation requires you to be brave enough to ask questions that would be considered rude and intrusive in other situations.

Make it easier for you and the witness. Address the probability of these questions at the outset. Mention it in the standard instructions you give the witness. Much of the embarrassment or discomfort that comes from a seemingly intrusive question can be traced to the surprise from the witness not expecting it. Also, if you discuss it before you begin the interview, you can answer any witness questions and preempt any problems.

You are a professional. Do not be reluctant to make the person uncomfortable. Your job is to find out the truth and make it hard for anyone to tell you anything less.

105) Accept a written statement to supplement the interview, but it shouldn't be necessary.

Many investigators welcome a personal statement, especially in theft investigations where the witness wants to unburden himself by telling all the facts. For most investigations, however, a personal statement is not needed.

If you ask probing, detailed questions, take detailed notes, and then prepare a memo with direct quotes, you have created a reliable business record documenting the witness's admissions of misconduct. A handwritten confession makes for good theater, but it is equivalent proof to the investigator's notes. In some cases, it may be more difficult to get again in writing from a witness what he has already told you verbally.

Approach the issue of witness statements instead as one of process fairness. There is no reason not to encourage a witness to submit his own statement. Sometimes witnesses seek the perceived security of describing events and issues in their own words. This reinforces process fairness (think about how it would look if you refused the witness's request.)

A written statement might also give you the opportunity to learn more about what may have happened. You may also spot contradictions (between the statements and his interview) and unknown motives that will spur further inquiries.

The personal statement, however, may turn out to be of little practical value. If the statement is little more than self-serving statements, you can simply disregard it as immaterial to the investigation. A witness uses the opportunity to provide the statement as a way either to repeat what you already learned in the interview or to offer written rhetorical flourishes such as how the witness has always striven to be the épitome of ethical behavior.

106) Joint interviews don't work.

Witnesses sometimes contradict each other. The situation may be a couple of "he said / she said" witnesses or multiple witnesses who saw the same incident. In the former situation, it might be tempting to put the witnesses in the same room and let them hash it out. In the latter, it could be an efficient way to substantiate what occurred. Either way, it is a bad idea.

Joint witnesses who are not adversaries might conform their testimony towards each other. However, if they disagree, your interview turns into a debate. If the topic is provocative, your interview may turn into a confrontation between your witnesses. The better approach is to interview each witness separately. Let the facts of each corroborate or undermine each other.

107) It rarely helps to tape an interview.

The only advantage of taping is that, of course, you have a verbatim transcript. But this comes at a price. You and the witness may become too self-conscious of the tape recorder. The witness may be unable to relax and give information, and you may be more concerned with sounding smart and asking good questions. Excellent note-taking is usually a better, easier and more-efficient choice.

108) "Should I get a lawyer?" Don't answer that.

An implicated person, once informed of the allegations, may ask if he needs a lawyer. This poses a problem that requires an immediate response. While everyone has the right to consult an attorney, your company also has the right to require its employees to disclose information relevant to the company's business. The conventional wisdom is to reply that only the witness should make that decision. Offer no opinion on whether the witness needs a lawyer. If you are an attorney, repeat that you are representing the company and cannot provide the witness with any legal advice. Your interview notes should state the substance of this exchange during the interview.

109) If asked, allow the witness to impose reasonable conditions.

An employee may also insist that an interview take place under certain conditions. These conditions might include (1) allowing other people in the room; (2) tape-recording the interview; (3) assurance that certain topics will not be discussed; or (4) assurance that the company will not disclose certain parts of the interview without that employee's prior consent. This situation requires both you and management to weigh the need for the information against the burdens imposed if the company agrees. If the company agrees to an accommodation in return for submitting to an interview, the agreement should be confirmed in writing.

Don't stand on ceremony. The witness may want something—such as a friend to sit there as a silent monitor—that really does not affect the quality of your interview. If you can accommodate it, just roll your eyes, play along, and get the information you need.

First, ask yourself why the witness thinks these conditions are needed. If you can learn what motivates these requests, you might be able to respond in a way that moots the request—suggesting the witness take notes himself may obviate the need for a friend in the room—or learn something else about the person.

110) "Am I in trouble?" You might be.

Once told of the investigation, employees often ask whether they are in trouble. Don't hedge the question—the only fair answer is "possibly." It is certainly possible that employees may be disciplined if they engage in misconduct, but at this point in the investigation you are just gathering the facts. Don't put yourself in a position where you have to eat your words if a seemingly innocent witness becomes implicated later. Transparency is key here. Honesty, even if the truth may be unpleasant, is the best policy. It also gives you credibility with the witness because, if you made the possibilities seem too rosy, the witness would likely not believe you anyway.

111) Practically speaking, employees cannot refuse to talk to you.

In the private sector, there is no Fifth Amendment right to remain silent. An employee cannot decline to speak to an investigator in the course of a proper investigation because he fears the information exposes him to discipline or termination.

Your company should have a "talk or walk" policy. This means that, as a condition of employment, each employee must cooperate with the inquiries of a valid company investigation. No one can be compelled to speak to you. However, an employee can be terminated for refusing to do so. (Your company must implement this policy. Otherwise, how will you compel people to submit to interviews?)

Many witnesses who refuse to speak actually fear something about the interview process. Try to learn about the basis for their refusal. You may find out that the witness fears retaliation or doubts your confidentiality. He may want to speak to you off-premises so that others do not see him with you. If you take the time to learn his concerns, you may find that you can alleviate them and get the information you need from him.

112) Let thy witness go.

You can't prevent a witness from leaving the interview room. Never lock the door, block an exit, or otherwise make a witness believe he is not free to leave at any time. You may expose the company to a false-imprisonment claim.

Your company's management empowers you to change that person's job responsibilities briefly in order to facilitate the opportunity for the interview. As a condition of his employment, the witness must cooperate with a workplace investigation. Every employee must assist his employer to maintain a safe workplace that is free of physical and legal hazards.

When an employee threatens to leave, simply explain that you will not prevent him from going. There should be no threats, no raised voices, and no excessive number of company representatives in the room. However, remind him that, as a company employee, he is required to submit to the interview. If he does leave, tell him that you will inform his supervisor immediately. The company cannot compel him to submit to an interview. The company, however, can terminate him for refusing. (Again, this might be a bluff either to distract you or get you to end the interview early.)

113) Assess the credibility of your witnesses.

If so much of the investigation depends on witness testimony, much depends on the quality of that testimony. Consequently, you must do more than just gather information. You must determine whether the information is credible. The more credible the witness, the more weight to be given to the information offered.

To determine credibility, you must first actively listen. Listening is much more than just concentrating. Listening involves perceiving what the witness is actually communicating.

To assess credibility, ask yourself the following questions:
- Was the witness present and aware during the incident?
- How well developed are the witness's powers of observation?
- Is what the witness is telling you logical? Does it make sense? (Truthful stories are logical. They do not appear to be scripted.)
- What was the witness's demeanor?
- Did the witness make contradictory statements?
- Did the witness have a reason to falsify what was said?

- Does the witness have any known or suspected bias?
- Does the witness stand to gain from the desired outcome?
- What are the witness's relationships to other witnesses and the subject of the investigation?

Remember to judge credibility. Information learned that appears relevant is useless unless it is also credible.

114) Have an "airplane rule."

When conducting interviews, accept the fact that people are generally nervous and may be evasive. Don't take it personally. For some reason, a witness may decide that lying is a better strategy than telling you the truth.

If you believe a witness is lying, first try to undermine factually what you believe are the untrue statements. If the witness refuses to change his position, confront him by telling him that you think he is lying, and that you understand he may believe it is better to lie about what happened. (Perhaps by exposing the falsity of what you are being told, the witness will see a futility in lying and give you truthful testimony.) Then remind him about the company's zero-tolerance rule about lying in a company investigation. Then tell him that he needs to think carefully about what he has stated and whether he wants to stay with that explanation and let the chips fall where they may.

You should always seek the information you need to complete the investigation. A witness who lies may do it through fear or even panic. Perhaps, if given some time to reflect, the witness may give you the truth. So give the witness a chance. Consider an interview to be completed once you step on the airplane to fly home. If the witness reaches out to you before then to change his information, consider it only to be a "refinement" of his past information. This way, he has some time to reflect, and you get accurate information, including possible admissions of wrongdoing.

If he maintains the untrue statements, and you can prove he lied to you, then the witness should be terminated for that reason alone, regardless of the outcome of the investigation.

115) It is possible to detect deception.

People are not usually complicated, and most of us are terrible liars. Even people who seem to lie effortlessly can be detected if you are alert.

We were each raised to believe that lying is wrong. To lie effectively, we have to give explanations that sound believable—we need to convince someone that the lie is actually the truth—but that contain the falsehoods.

When it comes to lying in an interview, its not just about sweaty palms and shaking legs. There are also common verbal patterns that might alert you:

- Deceptive witnesses tend to deny their wrongdoing specifically while the truthful person will deny the problem in general.
- Deceptive witnesses tend to avoid realistic or harsh language while the truthful do not.
- Truthful witnesses generally answer specific inquiries with direct and spontaneous answers. The answers are "on time" with no behavioral pause.
- Deceptive witnesses may fail to answer or delay answers. They may ask to have the question repeated or repeat the question asked. This allows them time to think of an answer.
- Deceptive witnesses may have a memory failure or have too good a memory.
- Deceptive witnesses tend to qualify their answers more than truthful persons.
- Deceptive witnesses may support their answers with religion or oaths. The truthful rarely employ this tactic.
- Deceptive witnesses tend to be overly polite and it is more difficult to arouse their anger. The truthful will be quick to anger and any denial will grow stronger.
- Deceptive witnesses may feign indignation or anger initially but will quit as the interview continues.

Effective use and interpretation of signs of deception requires training and practice. There are many variables, and these signs are only clues to spur closer questioning. Be wary of making decisions about witness veracity based only on your interpretation of the witness's body language, without some other form of evidentiary verification.

116) All lies are not the same.

Lying is not a natural human behavior. It must be learned. Liars lie for many reasons. Some know that lying works and doing so absolves them of the consequences of their misconduct. Other people lie because of fear. Admitting misconduct involves significant embarrassment. Consequently, there are enormous pressures to hide the truth, minimize the wrongdoing, and lie.

So now we know that witnesses do not lie because they dislike you. But the lie does not get you any closer to understanding what happened and what didn't, even if the lie itself can get the witness fired.

When you detect in an interview what you believe is a lie, the more effective strategy is to use the lie as an indicator of where to dig. The witness is not likely to lie about an unimportant issue, of course. So focus on that area.

To know where to dig, you have to understand the different types of lies because, although you have a clue as to the subject matter, you don't yet know how the implicated person factors into it. Lies generally break down into these types:

- **The simple denial**. This is the lie where the witness tells you he didn't do something the facts are showing you he likely did.
- **The lie of omission**. This is the lie where the witness leaves out embarrassing or incriminating information.
- **The lie of fabrication**. This is the lie where the witness invents the story. This lie requires the witness to use imagination and consistency in his attempt to persuade you it is the truth.
- **The lie of minimization**. This is the lie where the witness wants to downplay his culpability. A good example is the lie where the witness admits to stealing, but only a small amount rather than the large amount you think he took.
- **The lie of exaggeration**. This is the lie where the witness stretches a true fact to the point where it is a lie. A good example is the lie where the witness exaggerates about his former salary.

Finally, the detection of a lie is not the time for a "gotcha" moment. When it happens, first confirm that you understood the witness clearly, and that this was what he intended to say. Second, don't dwell on the topic but move to another one temporarily. (This may lead him to relax, believing that he has fooled you.) Eventually come back to the point and confront him with the details you know. Remember that a lie also leaves you with a factual contradiction the investigation must resolve.

On a related note, if you anticipate that the witness may lie to you, try to preempt it by hinting that you already know the answer to your key questions before you ask them. (Of course, this is most effective when interrogating the implicated person in the final stages of the investigation.) Boxing in the witness so he has no alternative but to give you the truth may be your most-effective path to understanding what happened.

117) If the implicated employee resigns, the investigation continues.

When the person accused of wrongdoing cannot be interviewed—for example, because he resigned or was terminated before you started the investigation, or he was interviewed but denied any wrongdoing—you must still complete the investigation. The investigation must proceed because the allegation has been made, there are still collateral risks to the business such as an endemic problem with other wrongdoers, and there may be flaws to be identified in business processes. Business-focused investigations are not all limited to specific inquiries about the conduct of specific employees.

There is an additional reason to continue your inquiries. The resigning employee may be trying to conceal criminal activity. Perhaps your investigation has only uncovered sufficient wrongdoing to justify termination. The employee thinks that by resigning, a closed investigation will not look deeper and discover the true harm caused to the company. It is entirely rational for an employee to do this if, by sacrificing his continued employment, he avoids a possible indictment.

One caveat though: If the investigation covered only personnel issues without bigger business implications, a resignation should terminate the investigation. There would be no added value to the company from continued inquiries.

118) There's always a reason why the implicated person did it. Find the back story.

As you prepare for the interrogation, consider the implicated person's possible motives for committing the wrongdoing. Did he do it for the money? To save his job? To impress someone? When you have some idea—even if it is only a working hypothesis—you can then steer the interview in that direction. This approach may facilitate a confession. An implicated person who has convinced himself, for example, that the cash he took from the accounts-payable department was only a loan is unlikely to admit that he "stole" the money because, however unlikely, he thinks he will pay it back.

Your initial remarks should include some explanation as to why an investigation was conducted and what leads you to believe that the implicated person committed the misconduct. It is not necessary to make accusations—in fact, it will probably chill the conversation—but you need the implicated person to understand that you are there for a reason, your interview is not just a "fishing expedition," and you are confident you have the incriminating information you need.

119) Always try to get a confession. It makes your job easier.

A good investigator always seeks a confession. The practical reality is that it makes your task easier. The accounts-payable clerk who admits he stole the petty cash but surely intended to pay it back some time in the future has still admitted stealing it. Even when an implicated person casts his actions in a less-sinister light, he is still admitting his misconduct.

Securing an admission of wrongdoing from the witness accomplishes three important purposes. First, assuming you can corroborate the information, it conclusively proves that misconduct occurred. Second, it avoids exposing the investigation findings to complaints that the evidence was insufficient or the proof was inadequate. Third, a confession allows you to obtain mitigating or explanatory information that might assist management in determining how best to respond to the matter.

But why would the implicated person confess? Who in their right mind would admit wrongdoing to an investigator? The truth is that people will confess if they believe that the confession benefits them more than saying nothing. There are generally three reasons why people confess:

- The implicated person thinks you already know he did it, and that you can prove his wrongdoing.
- The implicated person wants to put his own spin on the story in order to make his position more understandable and possibly less culpable.
- The implicated person feels guilty.

The investigator can facilitate the confession by offering a rationalization that helps the implicated person save face. So if you want a confession, you have to work to get one.

120) Speak to the implicated person even if you think it's a waste of time.

A fair process always gives the implicated person the opportunity to respond to the allegations. When you properly interview the implicated person, you fulfill any fundamental-fairness rights that he might enjoy, and if he admits to wrongdoing, the statement may be fairly used in the investigation. As to meeting the requisite burden of proof, an admission from the implicated person is always better than simply concluding circumstantially from the gathered information that the implicated person committed misconduct.

The key word in the preceding paragraph is "opportunity." The implicated person is not entitled to have an interview happen. So you need only offer reasonable accommodations for an interview to be taken.

In practical terms, this means you can budget time for him only during your business trip to the office to conduct on-site interviews (or he'll have to do it by phone). You don't have to accommodate any conditions on the interview that you wouldn't accommodate for another witness. Even though he is the person suspected of misconduct, he is not entitled to impose on you his subjective view of how the interview should proceed.

However, remember that an implicated person remains an important information source. He may substantiate his own misconduct even as he tries to explain it away. He may explain how others colluded with him (and perhaps you did not know that earlier). His information may spotlight the process failures that facilitated his misconduct.

There is a good chance the implicated person will deny any wrongdoing. If so, offer him the opportunity to assist the investigation to establish his innocence. The implicated person may say he is entitled to a presumption of innocence, so he is not obligated to help you. If this happens, you should agree with him. But then point out that his stance deprives the investigation of his possibly exculpatory information and leaves you dependent on the remaining sources. Does he really want to take his chances that, despite your efforts, the others collectively told you enough to exonerate him, and the available documents show he didn't do it?

Even if the weight of the information uncovered tends to substantiate the allegation, the investigation is not over until the implicated person is at least offered the opportunity to respond to the allegations.

121) An interrogation is not an interview. Remember the difference.

There are actually two types of interviews (but one of them has a name that seems redundant): investigative interviews and interrogations. You will sometimes use both types with the same witness, but most of the time you will use one or the other.

Technically, an investigative interview is a non-accusatory fact-gathering conversation to determine facts, sequences of events, or alibis, or to confirm information with a specific witness. The questions are generally open-ended, and the witness does most of the talking. If close-ended questions are asked, the investigator is usually trying to clearly establish certain facts or to confirm important details.

Other than the implicated person, virtually all of your witnesses will receive an investigatory interview. Your objective with those witnesses is to gather relevant information to determine whether the allegation can be substantiated. These facts can be gathered either by open-ended questions seeking narrative answers or close-ended questions to pin down key details.

The implicated person is generally interviewed last so he can meaningfully respond to the information you've gathered. (This is intended to solicit his responses, offer him the procedural fairness of being confronted by the information, and, it is hoped, to persuade him to admit his misconduct.) By the time you've reached the implicated person, the fact-finding phase is essentially complete.

An interrogation is not an inquiry for facts. It is a search for admissions and a confession. An admission by the implicated person—even with spin and mitigating circumstances—is still an admission. The additional information may put the misconduct into a factual context, but it is still misconduct. Your findings are always stronger when you can point to an admission than when you have no choice but to rely on the aggregate weight of the information you gathered. (It also gives you the peace of mind that you don't have to worry about being wrong.)

You obtain admissions by asking discrete close-ended questions that are intended collectively to constitute a confession. A close-ended question that simply asks, "Did you approve fake invoices to steal money from the company?" will generally receive an answer of "No."

Discrete questions will accumulate admissions to build a confession because they progressively paint the implicated person into a corner. Even if he continues to maintain his innocence, it's essentially a futile gesture. In an interrogation of the implicated person suspected of approving the invoices, for example, the discrete questions could proceed this way:

- You approved these invoices, right?
- Your approval means you saw the work performed or confirmed that it had been performed, right?
- Your signature appears on each of these invoices, right?
- This means the company should properly pay each one of these, right?
- But you don't know any of these consultants, right?
- And you don't know if the work was actually done, right?
- But you knew your signature was intended to make others rely on what you did so the invoices would be paid, right?

For each of these discrete questions, the answer is either yes or no. The answer is either an admission or a way you can paint him further into a corner until you get an admission. For example, if he denies that he doesn't know any of the consultants, ask him to tell you who they are. He probably won't or can't tell you.

The interrogation also looks for context and mitigating circumstances. Once again, most implicated people are not evil but are colleagues who made some bad decisions and likely compounded them with additional bad decisions. Learn about what motivated the misconduct so you can determine if any workplace factors—poor management, no perception of misconduct detection, a lack of training, etc.—facilitated it.

So even if you get admissions and possibly a confession, don't stop there if you can keep getting relevant information. You add true value when you can provide a full explanation.

122) Empathy is the easiest way to get an accused employee to confess.

The vast majority of implicated people get themselves in trouble through incompetence, poor training, insufficient supervision or making short-term decisions without considering long-term consequences. Regardless of what you may think, these people do not see themselves as bad people. If you seek a confession, it's his self-perception—however objectively distorted—that matters.

This approach is where your natural humanity plays a role. In other parts of your job, it can be a disadvantage. When seeking a confession, it becomes an advantage.

Entire books have been written on this topic, but in a nutshell: you can get someone to confess when you construct questions that characterize the person's conduct as he sees it. For example, a person who stole money may see it as a loan, as unlikely as it seems to you. That person will not admit to stealing, so questions asked from that perspective will fail simply because he does not consider himself a thief. That person, however, might admit to borrowing money that for some reason he has not gotten around to returning to the company. Either way, the admission works for you to show the misconduct.

A well-chosen theme offers the implicated person some rationale as to why an investigation was conducted and what led you to believe the implicated person chose to commit misconduct. The theme does not include making accusations. The investigator usually proposes that he believes the implicated person did commit misconduct. The investigator admits to the implicated person, however, that what is not then known is why the implicated person behaved as he did. In other words, you are not asking if the implicated person is guilty. You are asking *why* he is guilty.

People who are guilty of something frequently try to distance themselves psychologically from the offense. Theme development therefore makes a confession more palatable. The implicated person might have a moral—though not legal—justification for what he did. Morally acceptable themes like financial duress, an intention to pay the money back, poor employer treatment, etc. make it easier for an implicated person to confess. This further illustrates why it often pays to interview the implicated person last. Earlier witnesses may have given you details about the implicated person's possible motives and rationalizations, and this can help you construct an accurate theme in advance.

Perhaps it is just human nature, but most people consider themselves to be good. Even if we are candid enough to admit when we have done something improper, we are often quick to rationalize it away or blame external factors for leaving us with no alternative. No one will realistically tell you that he forged the accounts-payable checks simply because—with apologies to Willie Sutton—that's where the company keeps the money.

Theme development is not foolproof, however. People respond differently to life's challenges. There is no single way in which people handle problems. People do not go down the same road or take the same steps you might in a similar situation.

When you think you know why the implicated person committed the misconduct, the most important thing to remember is this: you don't understand. Accept that you don't understand why he did it. Accept that you don't understand how the challenges he was facing were sufficient to compel him to commit misconduct. Accept that you don't understand what alternatives were available to him. There is still a lot about human motivations that will remain a mystery to an investigator.

123) Take a second bite at the apple if needed.

When conducting interviews, you usually get smarter about the facts as the investigation proceeds. By the time you have completed the final interview, you should have a much better feel for what has occurred and the interpersonal dynamics that lay behind the actions of the people involved. Frequently, however, this means that you didn't ask your first witness all the questions for which you needed answers because, at the time, you were not aware of those lines of inquiries.

As the investigator, you are entitled to a second bite at the apple, so to speak. There is nothing wrong with either (1) re-interviewing the witness, (2) having a brief telephone conference to pin down the new details, or (3) asking detailed questions in an email for which you seek a written response. You goal should always be complete and accurate information. Not getting it all on the first try is no excuse to settle for an incomplete effort.

124) End each interview on a positive note.

Sometimes interviews go easily. You get a helpful and articulate witness who doesn't fear where you are going. Other times, a witness just gave you—or failed to undermine—the proof needed to get fired. Whatever the result, an interview should be closed on a positive note. Even if disturbing information was elicited, you can at least take an "at least we now know what happened" approach.

Don't forget that you may not get a second chance with this witness, and you need to be sure your information is valid. Use your closing remarks to review key information learned during the interview to be certain these points were correctly understood. In a contentious interview, you might even note that you recapped what you learned in case of a later recantation by the witness.

At the end of the interview, thank the witness for the information furnished. Give the witness your telephone number—better yet, leave your business card—if more information becomes available or is remembered. Keep the door open for future contact if he would like to add or change anything. The goal is to obtain the most accurate information possible. An interview is not intended to be a memory test.

Interviews are generally the most important fact-finding step. Never close the door to additional information or a chance to ask some supplemental questions.

125) Don't sell before the close either.

Salesmen seem to be a savvy bunch of people. The successful ones have a talent for reading people and understanding human nature. A common sales mantra is "don't sell past the close." This means that once you have obtained the customer's agreement to purchase the goods or services, stop negotiating. The risk of a continued discussion is that the salesman might say something that will inadvertently cause the customer to change his mind and cancel the deal. It is basically a rule of discretion.

For investigators, there is a corollary rule of "don't sell before the close." Under this rule, you should neither make assurances about what is likely to happen as the fact-finding proceeds nor about which witnesses are actually going to appear for their interviews. These assurances, if they don't materialize, may hurt either your credibility or your investigation planning (if you built your strategy around the witness's participation).

A useful example of the rule is when an investigator believes he has persuaded the implicated person, who had until that time seemed standoffish, to appear for an interview. The investigator now believes that he may likely obtain an admission or at least some incriminating information from the witness. At least the proof in the investigation will no longer be completely circumstantial. The investigator may also feel a sense of professional satisfaction because others had doubted whether the implicated person would ever consent to an interview even at the risk of his dismissal.

All of this is good, but what is he going to do when the implicated person, for some reason or another, does not appear as promised? Did he already tell the managers and others that he had secured her testimony? Did he take the understandingly human "victory lap" that he had achieved something others couldn't? Does he now look a little foolish as if he just got "played" by the witness?

When you have a difficult witness scheduled through some extra effort, there is nothing wrong with telling others that the interview has been tentatively scheduled. There is also nothing wrong with taking some quiet satisfaction from your apparent achievement. However, don't forget that you have not accomplished the interview until after you have actually taken it.

An implicated person is making a cost-benefit analysis when he agrees to an interview. Even if the interview was scheduled in good faith, the witness may later conclude that he will not be able to achieve the factual spin he thought was possible. A friend might have talked him out of it. He might have learned what information you've been gathering from other witnesses and concluded that you had him painted factually into a corner. Who knows?

Remember that the principle of "never say always, never say never" applies here too. Until all the questions have been asked and answered, you have not interviewed the implicated person. Don't assume that this will happen until it actually does.

126) Destroy your interview notes. Write a memo instead.

If you intend to rely on any of the information you learn in the interview, you must memorialize the witness's statements. Just as a relevant document taken from a filing cabinet serves as part of your findings, so should an interview memo. When prepared correctly, the facts contained in an interview memo stands as a reliable and credible piece of investigation evidence.

We are frequently busy as we investigate our own cases. We know what we recently heard from the witness. But there is a risk if you indulge the temptation simply to drop your handwritten notes in the file. Your notes are your subjective understanding of the matters you discussed. Notes are written in your unique shorthand. Problems start when others review your notes and draw different conclusions from what you intended. Worse, you may be asked to recall things that happened and not be able to decipher exactly or completely what you wrote.

If another person is taking notes for you during the interview, then the risks are compounded, especially the risk that the two sets of notes contradict each other. Either way, your investigation is, practically speaking, deprived of the precise information the witness offered. To make matters worse, you have now inserted yourself into the investigation process by having to act as some kind of interpreter to explain what the witness said in the interview. Stated another way, the value of this witness to your investigation findings now depends not on what he said, but rather on what you recall that he said. You are, essentially, now the witness to hearsay information.

You can avoid this problem. As soon as possible after the interview is completed, draft a simple memo to the file transcribing your notes into simple declarative sentences or a narrative of the conversation. Use as many direct quotes from the witness as possible. The memo must include all the substance from your notes. You cannot "cherry pick" the facts and answers you like (or consider relevant) and ignore the rest.

Do not write your interview memo in question-and-answer format. It makes reading it tedious, and you could be challenged as to why you asked a particular question and not another.

Then destroy your handwritten notes. The memo should be the sole written recollection of the interview. Through this process, you will also identify any gaps in your questioning that will require you to get supplemental information from the witness. You are also more likely to remember details that you left out of your notes but should be added to the memo. If for some reason you cannot decipher your notes, you will then be able to correct the situation quickly.

Make the interview memo a good one. If there is a lawsuit, a complaint to a regulatory agency or even an internal inquiry, the memo is going to be produced. If the witness is critical to your investigation findings, any scrutiny of your conclusions will include a scrutiny of that memo. Remember that the interview memo can be both a sword and a shield. A properly documented interview memo not only will justify a management decision but it can also protect you from a claim that the findings were unsupported or the implicated employee did not admit what he actually confessed to you.

A good interview memo can also prove a negative. For example, if a witness falsely claims that he said something in the interview that somehow favors his position, its omission from a proper, contemporaneously prepared interview memo is going to show that it is more likely than not that the statement was not made. This is another place where a consistent investigative approach protects you.

Some people argue that the witness should review the memo or sign it to signify that he agrees to its accuracy. There are differing views on this, but it is generally a bad idea. The memo represents your recording of information gathered from the witness. It does not represent a collaborative process between you and the witness. The information, if properly gathered, stands on its own even without the agreement of the witness because, presumably, he said the words your memo memorialized.

Your witnesses are not assisting you with the investigation process. Witnesses speak to investigators because they are compelled to. They are not sitting in that room to facilitate your note taking or help you complete your inquiries. Witnesses should be asked for their information and then allowed to go back to their lives.

Your notes are taken to assist you in preparing an interview memo. You should be trained and sufficiently attentive so that you can take accurate notes, whether or not the witness shares your confidence in your ability.

If you want to confirm the accuracy of your questioning, a better approach is to recap the major points with the witness. Then you note this step in your interview memo, which will also bolster the credibility of your memo. ("I asked the witness the question a second time, and he repeated the answer.") And if you misunderstood something, you can clear it up right there.

127) Opinions and editorializing don't belong in the interview notes.

Good interview notes are complete, accurate, and allow the investigator to recreate the substance in the interview memo. Notes do not contain any editorializing or opinions of the investigator. If the notes include things other than straightforward descriptions of facts, the objectivity, credibility or opinions of the investigator will be questioned as a way to neutralize the information in the memo.

You can convey the substance of your observations without crossing the line into editorials and opinions. Rather than write that "Bob seems impatient and disinterested," explain in your notes that "Bob frequently looked at his watch, asked how long the interview would take, and stated three times that the interview was a waste of everyone's time." This would be more accurate, and only your observations are possibly at issue, not your judgment and credibility.

128) The truth is logical.

You may sometimes get perplexed when trying to explain what happened in an investigation. The information learned may seem to have multiple explanations, and the situation is complicated further by witnesses who either spin the facts or inject their own speculation into the testimony.

So how do you know when you've uncovered the truth? There is no easy answer, but the good thing is that the truth is logical. Does one of the stories make more sense than the other? Can you confirm any facts which arose before or after the event? Were the people involved meeting or socializing with the people that would show that they were getting along fine before the "incident?" So rather than focus on the exactly what was said, pay some attention to the peripheral facts and see what you can learn.

129) A timeline puts everything in perspective because most of what we do is reactive.

When it comes to information, you are always the last guy at the party. The operative facts have likely all occurred. It is the rare investigation where relevant facts continue to develop after the investigation begins. So this regularly leaves you behind the factual curve and requires an expeditious inquiry.

As you assemble the facts, you'll need to organize them in some coherent way. The easiest way to organize this collection is by creating a simple timeline of relevant facts. Use the witness interviews as well as your documents. The chronology is a simple way to gather the information and keep the investigation focused.

As the facts are organized, you'll easily see important lines of inquiry to follow (for additional details as well as impeachment and gaps to fill in). As additional information is gathered, the timeline is supplemented with the new details.

130) It's rarely a good idea to have more than just you and the witness in the room.

Conduct your interviews one-on-one unless there is some compelling need to place another person in the room. (For example, if you anticipate a difficult interrogation, you may want someone in there who could back you up, explaining the questions you did and didn't ask.) The intimacy of just two people yields better information, especially when the witness is likely to explain things that could be embarrassing.

It is rarely helpful to have the witness's boss in the room, especially if the boss was the one who suggested it. In those situations, the boss is likely more worried about how the witness's information will affect him, and the boss is not necessarily focused on assisting your efforts.

Your goal is an efficient, productive interview. Don't organize the interview in ways that chill the conversation. You will face enough obstacles to getting as much detail as you need without creating more of them.

131) You don't need every shred of paper. It's quality, not quantity.

There is a common belief that you need to obtain every possible document so that you can peruse it for relevant information. Wrong. It will delay the completion of the investigation and probably distract you from the limited scope of the inquiry.

If you think about the allegation you are investigating, the elements of that allegation will come to mind. You only need enough documents (1) to tell the story of what happened, and (2) to meet your burden of proof—a preponderance of the evidence—regarding each element. That's all.

A document is only helpful if it is relevant. It is relevant only if it helps to prove an element of your allegation.

In a perfect world, you'd leave no stone unturned. Unfortunately, you don't have that luxury. So start with the documents you believe are most relevant to the allegation you are investigating, such as the personnel file, expense reports and payroll data. Look at the emails of relevant people for clues. Unless you fear the destruction of evidence, stick initially to the basics. You can always expand outward from there if and when the need arises.

132) In each investigation, some documents are better than others. Know which ones are best for your investigation.

Documents often give the clearest record of important events. Most documents are created at a time before the problem was uncovered. The facts discussed in the documents are usually accurate at the time they were created because there was no motive then to falsify or distort them.

Some documents are more helpful than others. Emails are terrific documents for workplace investigations. Emails give you snippets of the bigger story. And the ease of emails eliminates the time delay that used to allow cooler heads to prevail when sending angry notes. Consequently, an e-mail message may give you valuable insight into the real dynamics that were occuring at that moment in time, rather than the cautious recounting of events witnesses might tell you in an interview.

The documents you gather depend, of course, on the investigation you are conducting. Because every investigation is different, so is its document trail. However, there are some documents you will find useful in each investigation.

As a standard practice, consider obtaining the personnel file for your implicated person and your key witnesses. These files contain a number of useful documents. You will learn about the employee's biographical and work history. You will have signature exemplars that are likely valid (the employee probably signed these forms long before the misconduct occurred). The file will have past management appraisals which will show you how the employee has historically performed in your company. Finally, you will have the employee's compensation information.

This information is unlikely to affect your investigation issues significantly. But it can be very helpful when trying to establish the context in which the investigated conduct occurred.

133) Documents can do more than just establish new facts. Documents can support the ones you already know.

Besides establishing facts, documents can play a supporting role by providing important background information. Documents support the findings in a number of ways:

- They can help corroborate facts. "See, this email supports your statement that you were also at the meeting,"
- They can impeach. "If you didn't know about the impending deadline, how do you explain these emails where you were cc'd?"
- They can pin down crucial details. "This email recaps the meeting, which says it occurred yesterday. So the meeting was the 25th, right?"
- They can show issues being discussed. "The email lists the vendor's unpaid bills as one of the urgent topics, right?"
- They can establish time frames. "The email is from November, so it shows that this was an urgent issue back then, right?"
- They can identify witnesses and often what topics to cover.
- They can help you prove motive.
- Documents can be used to refresh memory even if the document itself won't be part of your proof. Showing an email with the witness's name in the header reminds the witness he was at the meeting.

- They can help you reconcile contradictions between two witnesses if a document shows accurate facts to correct someone's statements.

So when gathering documents, remember that they can have more uses than just as a freestanding source of facts.

134) You can't always get what you want. But you might get what you need.

When searching for documents, every investigator hopes to find the smoking gun that proves the misconduct and makes all the factual pieces fit. That rarely happens, however. Documents cannot be located. Emails may be deleted before the server backs them up. People may have had the foresight to avoid using the company data systems to which you have access.

But don't forget that you might still be able to piece things together circumstantially. The pieces, collectively, may satisfy the burden of proof. Or the pieces may be enough to convince an implicated person that it is now time to "come clean" and explain his wrongdoing.

For example, assume an executive is accused of a romantic relationship with one of his subordinates. If proven, this would be an impermissible conflict of interest. When confronted, the subordinate acknowledges their trysts. However, she explains that the two were discreet enough not to use the company email system. She does give you the approximate dates of their encounters.

In a perfect world, the IT department would retrieve romantic emails from the two of them, expressing their romantic feelings and plans. However, don't forget that there may be expense reports you can review and Outlook calendar entries, among other sources. This might be enough to overcome the denials of an executive who cannot imagine why someone would accuse him of this.

The point here is not to give up. If you cannot get the information directly, consider how you can assemble it indirectly. Even if the documents, knitted together and standing on their own, would not be enough to satisfy the burden of proof, they might be enough for an effective interrogation.

135) Evidence is information that reveals the facts, but all evidence is not the same.

Workplace investigations borrow many things from criminal and civil procedure. Because they handle employer-, not government-, driven processes, workplace investigators are not bound by courtroom evidence rules. So an investigator can rely on hearsay information, for example, when determining whether misconduct occurred.

The evidence rules are useful nonetheless. The rules contrast the different types of evidence and their suitability as proof. Some types of evidence are more reliable than others, and some are probative only if certain preliminary steps are satisfied. The evidence rules acknowledge that meeting the burden of proof is determined both by the quantity of evidence as well as its quality.

Here in a nutshell are the key evidence principles that you should know:

Types of evidence:

- Information from people can be testimonial or demonstrative (showing you a bruise). Information can be either based on personal knowledge or hearsay.
- Documents can be obtained just to prove their existence (there was a contract) or to establish the substance of its contents (the witness was the one who signed it).
- Physical objects may be used to prove their existence or identity (the serial number on the laptop shows that it once belonged to the company) or to demonstrate a physical characteristic (the door lock shows the nicks and marks of a break-in),

Qualities of evidence:

- **Relevance.** Does the evidence tend to make an important fact more probable than it would be without that evidence? If not, then it is not relevant. You should ignore irrelevant information.
- **Materiality.** Evidence may be relevant, but not all relevant information is material. Evidence is material if it proves or disproves an allegation. (Romantic emails between the boss and his assistant would be material in a sexual harassment case). Evidence is *relevant* if it tends to make a fact more probable. A fact is *material* if it tends to prove or disprove an allegation.
- **Competence.** Even if the evidence is relevant and material, it must still be competent. Do the circumstances in which the evidence was found support a belief in its truthfulness? For example, statements by a witness with a history of lying, or impaired perception, or with a strong bias or prejudice, are likely to be of limited value in establishing facts. Similarly, a confession or statement containing information contrary to one's interest or benefit obtained by coercion will not be as reliable as one obtained fairly and freely.

- Emails taken off your company's server would be competent.
- Statements by an employee with a history of lying or bias might not be.
- **Authenticity.** This evidence requirement applies to physical objects and documents. Is the evidence what it purports to be? Is the signature on the document really that of the person whose name is identified there? If there is a doubt as to its authenticity, you should not rely on it and seek out a more-reliable version.

Categories of evidence:

- **Direct evidence.** This is evidence that may tend to prove a fact directly. The witness has actual knowledge of the fact to be proved. The witness does not need to rely on facts he didn't observe. A witness who says: "I saw the CFO shred the documents when he thought no one was looking" is giving direct evidence.
- **Circumstantial evidence.** When you can't find direct evidence, the existence of the fact may be established because reasonable people can draw inferences from other facts. Circumstantial evidence is direct evidence of one or more facts that can be established indirectly because there is a logical relationship between them. A witness who says that she saw the CFO's personal wastebasket filled with shredded financial documents may be circumstantial proof that the CFO or someone with access to his office shredded them.

The distinction between direct and circumstantial evidence is important because circumstantial evidence leaves room for an alternate explanation. (What if the cleaning crew regularly consolidates paper in the CFO's basket—which is the biggest one on the floor—before packaging it for recycling?)

- **Fact vs. opinion.** Opinions are conclusions premised on facts and the interpretation of those facts. "I saw Jim and Bob shouting at each other, and Jim was red-faced" is a recitation of facts the witness observed. To say that Jim and Bob were angry at each other is an opinion based on the observed facts. The opinion might be accurate, but you cannot be certain. What if the two were practicing their roles for your company's talent show?

In general, be careful with opinion evidence. If you consider it, explore the basis for their opinions. People can give opinions about certain events they observe as part of their ordinary work duties.

136) Hearsay evidence is not admissible in court. Good thing you aren't there.

Although a witness can provide testimony about what he heard others say, it is considered hearsay if the purpose of that testimony is offered to prove the truth of those statements. Normally, a witness should not be used for hearsay evidence, and the statements should be solicited from the person to whom they are attributed.

The Federal Rules of Evidence—the rules that govern the admission of evidence in federal courts—define hearsay as "a statement, other than one made by the declarant while testifying at the trial or hearing, offered in evidence to prove the truth of the matter asserted." The rules further explain that evidence constitutes hearsay only if three conditions are present:

- the evidence is an assertive statement or act;
- the statement or act was made or committed out of court; and
- the evidence is being used to prove the truth of the assertion.

Unless all three conditions are satisfied, the evidence is not hearsay.

Workplace investigations can properly consider hearsay evidence as proof. By contrast, hearsay evidence is seldom admitted in a court proceeding unless it falls within one of the hearsay exceptions. Hearsay is generally not admissible because it is second-hand information, and the declarant is not available for cross-examination, by the opposing party or the court, to establish whether the statement may be properly relied upon. Consequently, hearsay evidence is less reliable, so courts are reluctant to admit it into evidence. Even though we can consider it, workplace investigations should give hearsay evidence less weight than if it were direct evidence.

You may base findings of fact and conclusions on evidence that would be hearsay in a judicial proceeding. You should still be cautious using this evidence, recognizing that you did not have an opportunity to test its reliability by interviewing the original source.

There are some exceptions to the hearsay rule, however. The exceptions exist because certain statements, although made out of court, are considered unlikely to be false. This means that when you use such information, you don't have to discount its value to your investigation.

The common exceptions are:

- **Statements against interest**. It is generally agreed that when people make admissions, or other statements they know are likely to be detrimental to their interests, they are less likely to be lying than when they protest their innocence. Similarly, it is generally assumed that when innocent people are accused of wrongdoing, they will deny it. Thus, Bob may testify in court that Joe told him he was the one who stole the company laptops, and this evidence may be used to prove the fact that Joe made the statement, to show Joe's state of mind at the time, and to prove the truth of the assertion itself. Similarly, Joe's silence when Bob accuses him of stealing may also be introduced through Bob to prove that Joe shot Jim, as could Joe's response that Bob was right.

To establish the implicated person's acceptance of another person's accusation by silence, you should attempt to obtain facts that would show the following:

- The statement was made in the implicated person's presence and was in the form of an accusation against the implicated person;
- The implicated person heard and understood the accusation;

The circumstances were such that an innocent person would deny the accusation; and

- The implicated person remained silent, or gave an evasive or equivocal response.
- **Business records.** When a document is offered to prove the truth of the statements in it, it is hearsay. But bringing in all the witnesses necessary to prove the statements in a document can be unduly burdensome. Most business organizations have an interest in maintaining accurate records of the normal business they conduct regularly. When certain indicators of reliability are present in connection with the creation of a business record, the "business record exception" to the hearsay rule may be invoked. In those cases, courts recognize that the business record may be more accurate than the memories of the people who originally created it.

To establish whether a record was created in the ordinary course of business, the investigator should attempt to determine:

(1) Whether the document was prepared by a person with a business relationship with the organization (usually an employee, but other people who have business dealings with the organization may also qualify);

(2) Whether the person who provided the information recorded in the document had a duty to report the information;

(3) Whether that person had personal knowledge of the facts or events recorded in the document;

(4) Whether the document was prepared at a time reasonably close to the occurrence of the events;

(5) Whether it is a routine practice of the organization to prepare documents of this nature;

(6) Whether the information recorded in the document is the type of information the organization would ordinarily record in the regular course of its business; and

(7) Whether the information is essentially factual in nature.

Note that the person who provides the document need not have personal knowledge of the information recorded in the document. In fact, that person usually does not have such information.

The bottom line about hearsay statements is that, although you are not prohibited from using hearsay evidence, you should give it limited value and use it with caution.

137) Know when to start. Know when to stop.

When, based on all the information you gathered, you believe it is more likely than not that each element of the allegation is proven or not, it's time to stop. On a more practical level, consider yourself done when you can coherently explain what happened, and each of the important facts fits the theory like the pieces of a jigsaw puzzle. When the facts all fall in line behind one explanation, then you are probably done. Otherwise, you should keep looking.

On a related note, if you have multiple implicated people, you must prove each element of the allegation against each one by a preponderance of the evidence. There is no guilt by association or implication, except where you can show that the people knowingly acted in collusion with each other.

138) You have to decide what happened.

Most investigations collect more information than is necessary to reach a conclusion. Some information is redundant; other information is not pertinent to a decision. Sometimes the information is conflicting. Deciding what information to treat as evidence and how to deal with it in the investigation report is important, because in cases where remedial or disciplinary action is a possibility, the decision to accept the conclusions in the investigation report is likely to be made only after an examination of all the evidentiary material in the file. If the report does not appear to fairly address pertinent evidence, its conclusions may be rejected. Some common issues include:

- Evidence considered, but not relied upon, should be discussed in the investigation report if it is likely that others would want to consider it, or question the completeness of the report were it not mentioned. This is critical when there is conflicting evidence.

- The failure to discuss and explain why one version of events is relied upon in lieu of competing evidence will cause readers who are aware of the conflicts to question the objectivity of the writer.

- Evidence that is redundant or repetitive can be summarized when it comes from various sources that present no unique information. For example, stating that five people saw the implicated person in the office on a particular day is adequate in most cases.

- Testimony may prove difficult to analyze in some cases. Often, only a few witnesses have the entire story. The investigator must piece together fragments of the story to present the entire picture. Summarizing the testimony of witnesses providing these fragments is one acceptable technique to make the sequence of events clear. In complex cases, or cases with many witnesses, it is helpful to use some system for identifying what each witness said about each allegation, such as an evidence matrix or an outline.

The evidentiary analysis must bring together all documentary, physical, and testimonial facts relating to the allegations to reach a conclusion. The facts relied upon to reach each conclusion should be apparent to the reader. When the applicable standards are themselves vague, or the testimony conflicts, the reasoning that leads to a conclusion is not always apparent. In that case, the analysis in the investigation report must explain to the reader how the investigator reached the conclusion.

Don't forget to consider the "root cause" of why something happened. The root cause may be presented by showing that the implicated person didn't know the rule, could not comply with it, and/or would not comply with it.

139) At the end of the investigation, there are only three outcomes.

Considering the stakes involved, you have to make a finding. It is neither professional nor helpful to your company if you remain perplexed and simply shrug your shoulders as to the investigation outcome. You must make a decision, and there are only three possibilities:

- **Substantiated**. A substantiated finding results when a preponderance of the evidence supports the allegation of misconduct. The facts, from documentation and testimony, indicate that a violation occurred.
- **Unsubstantiated**. An unsubstantiated finding results when a (1) preponderance of the evidence supports the conclusion that the alleged misconduct did not occur, or (2) the available evidence is insufficient to meet the burden of proof, even if you believe that the misconduct occurred.
- **Inconclusive**. An inconclusive finding results in the rare situation where you simply cannot complete the investigation, for example because of the lack of availability of witnesses and/or documents.

140) The investigation report is your most important document.

Report writing is a necessary function of all investigators. Even if you consider it drudgery, you must do a good job.

Reports are where all the parts of your investigation come together. For example, good reports come from good notes. If the best investigation findings come from the best interviews, then the quality of your investigation will depend on the quality of the memos. The same holds true for selecting the right documents that substantiate or corroborate material details.

An investigation report must straddle the need for a full explanation of the relevant facts while not creating a document that admits company liability. Admitting liability, however important it is to not do inadvertently, is not the same as creating it. (This is the distinction the in-house lawyers tend to overlook.) An investigation report is not a primary document. The report is based on primary sources like witness interviews and company records. If there were a lawsuit over an issue you investigated, each of these witnesses may be deposed, and each of these records may be produced. So the report itself does not create any facts for an adversary to use.

But you can put the company at risk if the report is not drafted properly, and you offer more than just facts. The report should not contain any editorializing or legal conclusions. There should be no assessment of potential company liability. There should be no adjectives or adverbs that could be interpreted as your view of the company's exposure. And, of course, your personal views should never be included under any circumstances.

As a strategic move, have a discussion with your executive leadership regarding the proper role of your reports. You may find out that they would have a preference for seeing the business improvements that come from a robust, yet responsible, explication of the facts, rather than some memorializing document that does not allow them to fix the business.

The form of the investigation report depends on its intended use. There is no one-size-fits-all, and the better reports are tailored to the company's specific goals and needs.

A good report format includes an executive summary. The summary is a concise synopsis of the entire contents of the report. Depending on the scope of the investigation, the executive summary should not usually exceed three or four paragraphs. (The executive summary also acknowledges that senior managers often haven't the time or inclination to read the full report. You are better off respecting the amount of time your reader is likely to give your report.)

Although a good final investigation report details the process by which you investigated, don't emphasize process over substance. The process is simply the means by which you developed the facts. The substance is what your customers need from you. They should trust that your process was fair, thorough and professional without you laboring the point. The relative merits of your process are immaterial unless it yields a valuable substantive result.

141) The investigation report deals only with the precise allegations.

The investigation report should be explicitly limited by the scope of the investigation. The scope should be clearly specified in the report. The report's recommendations and findings should be limited by that scope as well. This will provide a clear understanding to anyone to whom the report is disclosed regarding the investigation's limitations. Later on, as additional facts develop, you may need to explain why the findings did not cover the areas under scrutiny. Without a scope specified, your investigation may look incomplete or incompetent because it will otherwise appear that issues and topics were ignored.

This is not an insignificant point. Investigations focus on specific areas like misconduct and process improvement. The investigation is not intended to resolve and/or critique each collateral issue as well. But remember that someone may be thinking—or hoping—you will do that. Specifying the scope sets that part straight.

Similarly, much of the information you dutifully gathered in the interviews will, in hindsight, prove immaterial to the investigation. (If you substantiated that a manager regularly stole from the company, the additional allegation that he was an irrational tyrant to his subordinates no longer seems needed.) Topics once thought pertinent can be inconsequential. No big deal. Like with movies, an investigation report benefits from careful editing.

142) The most important question to answer in the investigation report is why.

There is much to be said about what an investigation report should look like. Reports come in a variety of formats. Reports can be formal reports or informal memos. Reports can be chock full of details, citations and facts. It all depends on the specific goals of the investigation and the needs of your company's management.

If you check books, guides and online sources, you can learn all you need to know about what to include. Of course, ask your management—the ultimate customer of your efforts. This is an essential step too many compliance professionals forget.

However, regardless of what you read or any manager tells you, the single most important question to answer in your report is "why." Why did the implicated person do it? Why did he think it would not be detected? Why did he think it was acceptable, condoned or permitted? Why did he do it even though there are compliance training programs and company policies against it? Why did he feel entitled or think it was necessary to commit the misconduct?

Ask and answer these questions, and your report will truly add value to understanding what happened, how to address it, and how to prevent it in the future.

143) An investigation report is not a data dump. Think before writing.

If the investigation report will cover any sensitive areas, consult your company's legal department first. At least in the most sensitive areas, and in any preparation for litigation, the company may take steps to permit it to assert the attorney-client and other privileges. But remember that you are part of a business process. These risks must also be balanced against the benefits to the business if a detailed report leads to corrective steps. You can and should be able to walk this tightrope of competing priorities.

Do not offer conclusions in your report. You are just a presenter of facts. If you are tempted to offer a conclusion, it is probably because your investigation report is not clear enough, and you are trying to help the reader along to the conclusion you are trying to reach.

Similarly, don't insert opinions in your investigation report. If doubt is later cast on the validity of your opinion, then that doubt will undermine the credibility of the report and the underlying investigation. Focus instead on what the facts show, rather than your own personal insights, however valid and accurate they might be.

144) Show the good and the bad.

As an objective fact finder, you must show both the good facts and the bad ones. A common fault in investigation reports is the failure to document findings of no fault, no loss, or no wrongdoing. It is just as important to back up your findings with "positive" documentary evidence as it is to document adverse findings. The report that reaches a conclusion of no fault, no loss, or no wrongdoing must include sufficient documentation to show that the evidence supports that finding.

Simply put, you should be as interested in establishing innocence as in establishing guilt.

145) Offer no recommendations on discipline, compensation of aggrieved parties, etc.

A proper investigation report offers no recommendations on how an offending employee should be disciplined, whether the company should compensate someone, or similar possible post-investigation actions. Those steps are beyond the scope of the investigation. This is for a good reason. If you can decide on the resulting disciplinary action to be taken, a conflict of interest may be created that interferes with your ability to find the objective truth of what happened. The investigation report, however, may include recommendations for additional investigation and corrective changes to the business's operations.

Making disciplinary recommendations creates the appearance of a conflict of interest. If you conclude an investigation by stating that a certain disciplinary action is warranted, someone may argue that you skewed the investigation findings to support the punishment you advocated. Similarly, by offering recommendations, you may influence the decision-maker. In doing so, you might place your credibility in jeopardy.

As the fact-finder, you are probably in the best position to explain what happened, what didn't happen, and who did what. Nothing prevents you from being a source of information to the people who have to make the disciplinary decisions. Managers generally know what to do once they are properly armed with the facts.

What if you made a recommendation that was ignored (for example, the star salesman was not fired for harassing his secretary)? If the salesman committed the same misconduct in the future, your declined recommendation would help a plaintiff in a future lawsuit show that the company chose to ignore the person who knew the facts best.

You also may risk some credibility with the business people. If they do not want to follow your recommendation, will they try to avoid you next time, lest you again propose something they do not want to do?

In contrast, however, it is entirely appropriate to offer recommendations about process improvements if your findings discovered deficiencies. But this, too, requires some caution. Don't recommend fixing what isn't broken. Don't just opine that some process needs improvement without suggesting, at least as far as your facts show, what specific improvement would help. Most importantly, do not judge the people who created the process in the first place. Policies are made by bright men and women getting together and trying to do the right thing. You have the opportunity to give insight into how things really work in your company, so don't mess it up.

The reality is that properly developed facts will likely steer the business people towards the outcome you might recommend if you had the chance. If you are inclined to see some outcome occur, do an even better job developing a complete set of facts.

If your job duties require you to make such a recommendation, get a second opinion when making the recommendation. Knowing—and documenting—that someone else reviewed your findings and agreed with your recommendation significantly reduces the conflict-of-interest risk. And if your colleague does not agree with your recommendation, make the necessary adjustments to ensure a defensible result.

Similarly, investigators whose duties include making recommendations should place certain safeguards into the process. These safeguards include:

- The investigation is conducted according to an investigation protocol and established processes (not personal agendas).
- The investigation report clearly defines the investigator's role and the limits of his authority.
- The investigation is controlled by a specified scope and objective.
- The investigator and the investigation are subject to the oversight of a higher authority, like outside counsel or the CEO.

- The investigator is required to include in the investigation the implicated person's response to the information gathered as well as any information on mitigating circumstances.
- The investigator is bound to the standard of proof.

Safeguards like these reduce the ability—as well as the appearance of ability—for an investigator to pursue his own agenda, spin facts, and influence the decision-maker. If the implicated person later sues the company, it will be the investigation and not his misconduct that will be challenged at trial.

146) The reporter deserves a reply when the case is closed, but be careful what you say.

Reporters have no inherent right to know the outcome of an investigation or to see the investigation report. However, it may be a good practice to inform the reporter that an investigation was conducted.

The reporter should be told (1) that an investigation was conducted, (2) the investigation has been completed, and (3) your findings will be shared with management. The reporter is not really entitled to know more than that.

This may sound unfulfilling, but it is the safest route. What are you going to do if the reporter starts pressing you for information or complaining that "justice" will not be served? You might wind up saying something you'll regret later.

If the reporter is a company employee, he will probably see the outcome first-hand. If his complained-about coworker does not show up on Monday morning, he will know how the investigation worked out.

The bottom line is that reporters and witnesses have no greater right either to know the outcome of an investigation or to review the report more than do members of the general public.

147) Give read-outs if you don't trust them.

Because you are ultimately trying to improve the company, your job is not complete when you close the investigation. Your job is complete when, if applicable, any process improvements are made so the business runs better. The process improvements depend on accurate information. What do you do if you don't trust the people involved to convey your information accurately and without some spin that exonerates the person explaining it?

Assume you had a case where everyone in the office had been finger-pointing at everyone else, accusing each other of some flavor of misconduct.

Each person was convinced his or her assessment of the others was correct, and no one's good faith could be presumed. Your investigation findings, if delivered by someone else, would either be spun or, even if explained accurately, might be perceived as having been spun.

If this situation arises, there is a simple solution. The department staff should be assembled. Coordinate the statement of your findings with the department manager. Your findings should not be tailored to his needs, of course, but the read-out should provide the factual basis for the boss's segue into the steps intended to remedy the situation. This will allow the findings to serve as both a factual foundation as well as the business justification for the changes the boss intends to implement.

As part of your preparation, anticipate tough questions from those assembled. You will need to demonstrate a level of composure and tact that is beyond normal expectations. The measure of the character of an investigator is how effectively he is able to handle legitimate and illegitimate feedback on his investigative skill or the quality of the particular case. You should always be open to feedback in order to increase future case quality and avoid unfounded attacks.

148) Call the cops after the investigation is complete.

Although your executive management may want to contact the police as soon as they believe some law was broken, this is not an effective strategy.

Law enforcement agencies operate in a world of limited resources, shifting priorities, and real-life victims. There is no way they can investigate every case they receive. A past survey by the Association of Certified Fraud Examiners estimated that 78 percent of fraud cases reported to law enforcement go uninvestigated. There are just not enough resources to get to it all.

The most-effective strategy is to complete your investigation and develop your findings in a way that shows the police clearly and convincingly that a crime was committed. Prepare a detailed memo showing how, among other things, the misconduct cannot be explained other than as criminal activity. Attach and cite the business documents and interview memos that support your findings. In other words, "gift-wrap" the investigation for the police.

An approach that essentially leaves it to the police to figure out what happened to you will never bring effective results. Help yourself first, and then, it is hoped, they can help you.

If you focus on the criminal aspect, don't miss the most important aspect of workplace investigations—helping the business. Even when former employees are prosecuted, the victory is usually a Pyrrhic one because these people are usually judgment-proof and negotiate plea bargains. Instead, focus on what the bad guy's actions showed you about where your business needs improvement.

Bottom line: criminal conduct is the exception in your investigation findings. Focus instead on business-process failures and employee incompetence.

149) Litigation is not always the next step after an investigation is completed.

Litigation is not an investigation objective. Fact-finding to substantiate an allegation of misconduct is your objective. Litigation is something that occurs, if at all, once your objective has been met. Litigation is costly, time-consuming, and the chances of financial recovery are poor. Decisions to litigate are often made reflexively, with a desire to right a wrong, and/or a need to send a message to competitors.

The possibility of litigation later on is always something to consider, especially if the misconduct is likely to lead to someone being fired. However, the focus should be on identifying the misconduct and fixing the business problem that may have facilitated the misconduct.

A good investigation and a good report serve both the company's internal needs as well as the decisions about whether to file a lawsuit. Do a good job. Leave the litigation decisions to others.

150) You can't hide behind the lawyers when you investigate.

Investigations are rarely covered by the attorney-client privilege. In almost every case, the documents, statements and reports of an internal investigation are discoverable in a later lawsuit. The attorney-client privilege generally does not apply because that privilege, among other things, covers confidential discussions for the purpose of obtaining legal advice. Workplace investigations serve many goals, but legal advice is generally not one of them.

The rare occasion for which an investigation may be done under privilege is where your company lawyers have asked you to conduct an investigation to enable them to give legal advice to the company, such as where the company may be at risk for a lawsuit. In these cases, the investigation is not compliance-related, but is just fact-finding to assist the lawyers. If this should ever occur, make sure to get something in writing from the lawyers at the outset to memorialize that you are investigating at their request and to assist them.

Your work always looks different when it is an attached exhibit to someone's court complaint or when it is on an overhead projector in a courtroom. It certainly dispels the usual drop-it-in-the-file approach to most of our cases.

Investigate and write as if it is going to be reported in the *New York Times*. Nothing is protected from the use—and misuse—by an adversary, especially your notes. Each of your documents must be freestanding so that understanding them does not depend on some other documents or external knowledge. And, above all else, keep yourself out of the document.

Conclusion

I wrote this book to help you become a good investigator. The nature of the investigations business is that the better you become, the higher your company profile will be. But your desire to be a successful investigator presents you with a dilemma: If you are a timid investigator, you are ineffective. But if you are bold, you expose yourself to professional risk.

This book presented "protect your career" as its first part. Just like a police officer's first obligation is to go home alive at the end of his shift, your first obligation is not to jeopardize your job by becoming collateral damage to an effective compliance program. Despite their respective contributions, your colleagues who write codes of conduct, hang posters in lunchrooms, or pass out cafeteria cake on Compliance Day do not take the risks you must take in order to be successful.

So this book has not been primarily about interviews and documents. This book is more honestly about how you walk the tightrope between professional success and disaster.

This book concludes with some pearls of wisdom that come from my experiences in conducting over 300 workplace investigations. Here are my "Rules for Investigators:"
- There are only two grades in investigations: A and F.
- The way to do well is simply to do well.
- There is no "silver bullet" to a good investigation. There is only hard work and creative thinking.
- Use both your heart and your brain. An effective investigator needs both.
- Ours is a volatile business. Things go wrong all the time.
- Never say always, and never say never. You'll be regularly surprised.
- You aren't their friend, but you also aren't their enemy.
- Dare to be infamous. Investigations can be a dirty business.
- The only good faith you can believe in is your own.
- Nothing good happens to the people who work with you. The best that can happen to them is nothing.
- You will learn quickly who your friends are.
- It's business, not personal.
- You aren't the morality police, so don't take yourself too seriously.

- You can't afford to be cynical, but you also don't get the luxury of being idealistic.
- Your first obligation is to the truth, not pleasing someone in your company.
- Perception is reality.
- You will make mistakes. Just be sure to learn from them. Never be risk-averse in your decisions for fear of making a mistake.
- If you have a private prejudice, keep it to yourself. But remember that you are human too.
- You are in the risk-assessment, not the risk-taking, business.
- You must be and be seen to be above suspicion. Set the right example.
- Don't think of yourself as indispensible to your company. As Charles de Gaulle said, the cemeteries are full of indispensible men.
- Take full ownership of your investigation and every step you took or chose not to take. Use the "you're damn right I did" standard.
- Take a 360° view of your actions to preempt potential allegations against you.
- Be careful what you say. People might actually listen to you.
- Don't look for a bad guy. When given the choice between incompetence and intentional wrongdoing, bet incompetence every time.
- The usual explanation exaggerates rationality and conspiracy, and underestimates incompetence and fortuity.
- There is no "off the record."
- Each case has a "back story." Your job is to find it.
- Learn to say "I don't know." If used when appropriate, it will be often.
- Learn something from each case and always seek to be a better investigator.
- If you are not criticized, you may not be doing much.
- If in doubt, don't.
- Don't question business decisions as if you're the CEO of your company. The company has only one, and it isn't you.
- It's easy to assign blame in an investigation. It's much harder to understand what the subjects were thinking when they did it.

- It's not what you think happened. It's what you can prove happened.
- The first information you get is almost always wrong.
- If you have trouble getting the information, there's usually trouble with the information.
- Substance is always more valuable than process to your company.
- Don't just tell what happened. Explain what happened.
- What didn't happen is sometimes more important that what did happen.
- The truth is logical. Lies rarely make common sense when you scrutinize them.
- No one reports misconduct out of good corporate citizenship.
- If you act like you're ready for battle, you'll likely end up in one.
- Plan your investigation effectively and, when necessary, change it decisively.
- Never rush to judgment. Allow the truth to catch up to you.
- At the end of the fact-finding, make a decision. "I don't know" is not a decision.
- Find the misconduct. You don't want guesswork on your conscience, and playing with people's careers is not what you were hired to do.
- How you report your findings announces your priorities to management.
- Be precise in fact-finding and report writing. A lack of precision is dangerous when the margin of error is small.
- Accept that there will usually be blood on the floor when you are done. If misconduct occurred, heads are going to roll, possibly even to someone who might only be tangentially involved.
- Be prepared to defend everything you do. Your job may depend on it. When trouble finds you, the first time you lose an ethics claim may be the last one you'll ever fight. As the cops say, "don't pick up a nail."
- Regularly give yourself a *Miranda* warning: Everything you say or do in an investigation can and will be used against you.
- Slow down, think strategically, and take cover.

So keep looking for the truth. Be bold. But be careful.